Wakefield Press

THE NAVY-BLUE SUITCASE

Sally van Gent has lived in twenty houses across the globe, but with handmade rugs, Arabian coffee pots and an assortment of dogs, each one became home. She finally settled on ten acres in the Bendigo bush where she planted a heritage apple orchard, the subject of her first book, *Clay Gully.*

Also by Sally van Gent

Clay Gully

THE NAVY-BLUE SUITCASE

Curious Tales from a Travelling Life

Written and illustrated by

SALLY VAN GENT

Wakefield Press

Wakefield Press
16 Rose Street
Mile End
South Australia 5031
www.wakefieldpress.com.au

First published 2016

Edited by Julia Beaven, Wakefield Press
Cover designed by Stacey Zass
Cover photographs © LiliGraphie, Olga Pink, honglouwawa, Reinhold Leitner
Illustrated and designed by Sally van Gent
Typeset by Clinton Ellicott, Wakefield Press

National Library of Australia Cataloguing-in-Publication entry

Creator:	Gent, Sally van, author.
Title:	The navy-blue suitcase: curious tales from a travelling life / Sally van Gent.
ISBN:	978 1 74305 406 2 (paperback).
Subjects:	Gent, Sally van – Childhood and youth. Gent, Sally van – Travel. Travelers – Australia – Biography. Travelers' writings.
Dewey Number:	910.4

Contents

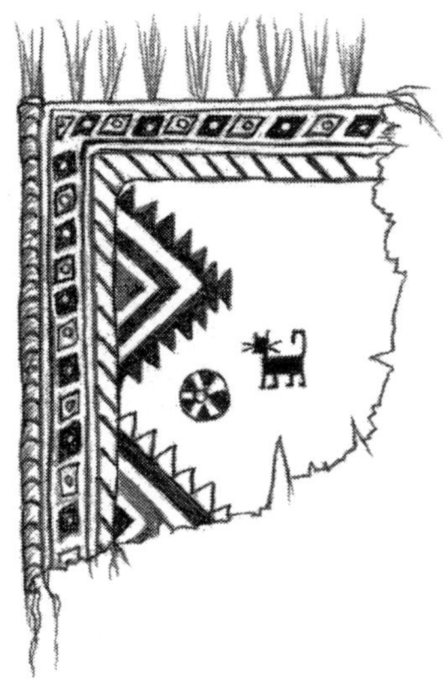

THE LIMES

The navy-blue suitcase

It must once have been a thing of beauty, but age had frayed its cream-silk lining and tufts of furry leather escaped the seams. It lay underneath our bed from the time we first moved into my grandparents' house and I knew all along it wasn't so much stored, as hidden there.

One evening I burst into our bedroom and caught my mother on her knees in front of the open case. In an instant she slapped down the lid and pushed it back into the darkness and blanket fluff.

I shared the big half-poster bed with my mother, and after she tucked me in each night she drew its heavy tapestry curtains. My grandparents' mahogany furniture framed the room – massive wardrobes with drawers so wide it took two people to open them. They contained our clothes and my grandmother's bed linen, but little else. My mother owned few personal possessions and those she had she kept inside her navy-blue suitcase.

It was years before I decided to look inside and only opened it then because I thought I might find something to help explain my father's odd behaviour. I waited until my mother had gone shopping and my grandmother was in the garden picking runner beans. Then I sneaked upstairs and pulled out the case from under the bed.

I'm not sure what I expected to find, but I was disappointed when I saw birthday cards and old letters held together with elastic. I glanced through them and set them aside. My fingers dug deeper and I came upon an ageing wedding photograph mounted on brown card. Three rows of guests smiled stiffly for the photographer – men in wing collars and women wearing cloche hats. The bride, swathed in an enormous veil, carried a bouquet of arum lilies with ribbon twisted around their stalks. The happy couple were flanked by four adult bridesmaids wearing capes over tucked satin dresses. I didn't recognise anyone in the picture and wondered why my mother had bothered to keep it. Perhaps it was the wedding of an old schoolfriend?

Then I noticed the flower girl. She was leaning against the knee of a woman who looked vaguely familiar. I studied her face. She must have been much younger then, but it was definitely my grandmother. I looked again to see if there was anyone else I knew, and made a second discovery – the bride was my mother! But whose arm was she holding?

It wasn't my father's.

Suddenly overcome by guilt, I pushed the photograph back under the letters and cards. Then I sat down on the edge of the bed and gazed through the window at the fields that stretched beyond our garden. Why didn't my mother tell me about this wedding? Who was the plump, broad-shouldered man she married so long ago? And what of my father, who came to visit us at Christmas?

There was the sound of the front door opening and I heard my mother call out, 'I'm home!'

I leaped up. Had I left the case exactly as I found it? I closed the lid, pushed it back under the bed and hurried downstairs. My mother was in the hallway, taking off her hat. I hesitated. I dearly wanted to ask about the photograph. But how could I, without admitting to poking around in her personal belongings, tucked away in the navy-blue suitcase?

The Limes

My grandparents named their house The Limes, for the two bright-leaved trees that leaned out over the front fence. Under their dappled shade grew tiny violets, lily of the valley, Christmas roses and Solomon's seal.

Between the trees and the coal shed was a dark and secret place where in the daytime fairies played among the fallen leaves, and at night climbed the stalks of the foxgloves to sleep inside their flowers. They were too shy to come out when I was near, but on windy days I heard them whispering.

There was always something good to eat in our garden: raspberries and apples, gooseberries and plums, cabbages and beans. And we were never short of honey for the fruit trees were pollinated by Grandpa's bees. He and I dug and planted together, and my cats, Timmy and Snowy, listened carefully while he taught me the Latin names of all his flowers.

Sometimes a hedgehog ambled into the garden for a saucer of milk and on rainy days frogs came out of their hiding place under the privet hedge and hopped around on the front path.

When my ball fell into the pit by the cellar window, I peered into it and counted five little frogs trapped in the bottom. To reach them I needed to move a heavy metal grate. As I pulled it aside the edges cut into my fingers and made them bleed. But I retrieved my ball and rescued the frogs that had turned snow white in the darkness.

On the last day of June, fifteen, and sometimes as many as twenty, of my schoolfriends came to the house to celebrate my birthday. They arrived in bathers and ran around the lawn under the hose. We splashed each other with water from buckets and bowls, and Grandma's old iron peggy-tub that she used on washdays for soaking the clothes.

Afterwards we sat down to one of my mother's marvellous birthday teas: boat-shaped sandwiches with paper sails, halved apricots on white blancmange made to look like poached eggs, and brown rabbit mousse on green grass jelly.

The visit

The door of the telephone room creaked open and a moment later my mother skipped into the kitchen, her cheeks all pink.

'That was your father,' she announced. 'Wonderful news! He's coming for Easter. He'll be here by lunchtime tomorrow.'

Grandma's eyes widened. She stopped in the middle of working the creases into the legs of Grandpa's trousers and laid down her iron.

'But it's Good Friday and the shops are closed. What are we to do? I'll have to ring the butcher first thing in the morning to see if he has a piece of sirloin. And we'd better get some cheese – Stilton. You know how much Waldo likes that.'

She dumped the part-ironed trousers on top of a pile of shirts lying in the laundry basket and folded up the ironing board. 'The rest of the washing will have to wait. What do you think about apple pie for dinner on Sunday?'

She turned to me. 'Sally, look in the cupboard and see how we're off for sugar. I'm going to make a batch of my special biscuits.'

She swept the plates into the sink, powdered the kitchen table with flour, and was soon kneading the pastry for her apple pie. Meanwhile, my mother dragged the vacuum out of the cupboard and started work on the hall carpet, while I was sent into the back room to dust the ornaments on the mantelpiece.

I hated housework. No sooner had I settled comfortably into a corner to read than my grandmother would call out, 'Where's that girl? Head in a book? Tell her to come into the kitchen and do something useful.'

That day though, excited as I was at the thought of my father's visit, I was willing to do whatever she asked. Once the dusting was done, I brushed the cat hairs off the armchairs, then wiped the hearth and polished the brassware till it glowed like the sun.

After a while my mother released me and I escaped into the garden.

I found my grandfather in the shed behind the greenhouse, potting up geraniums. 'Daddy's coming tomorrow,' I told him.

He grunted. 'You'd better help your mother carry the camping bed down from the attic then. You're going to need it.' He turned away and went back to teasing out the roots of his cuttings, readying them for replanting into bigger pots.

I watched for a while, waiting for him to say something else, but when he didn't I understood he wasn't as thrilled as I was about my father's visit. Mildly disappointed, I wandered back outside.

The Michaelmas daisies were in flower in the front garden and I bent down to pick a few. As I was arranging the pink and mauve clusters into a posy I thought about the last time my father visited us. It was at Christmas – not the one most recently gone, but the one before that. I remembered how happy I'd been to see him, and how sad I was when he didn't stay long enough to watch me open my stocking.

He did bring me a present though. After he'd kissed my mother and shaken hands with my grandparents, he went into the back room and settled into the armchair beside the fireplace.

'Come here, Sally,' he said, reaching for my hand and drawing me to his knee. 'Have you been a good girl while I've been away?'

'Yes,' I whispered, thrilled by his closeness: the scent of his shaving lotion, the oil on his slicked-down hair, the new leather smell of his shoes.

'Have you been working hard at school?'

'Yes, Daddy,' I said, shy and proud at the same time. 'I came top of the class in last term's exams.'

'In that case, I have a present for you.' He reached over the arm of his chair, picked up a flat white box and held it out to me.

'What is it?' I asked.

'It's a cake.' He laughed, and I knew he could tell from my expression that I was disappointed. 'Aren't you going to open it?'

I laid the box on the floor, carefully lifted the lid, and was surprised to see several layers of pink tissue. When I pushed them aside I discovered my father had tricked me, for instead of a cake I found a dress.

Its puffed sleeves were edged with ribbon and the bodice, drawn together by rows of smocking, was embroidered with tiny daisies. That was no ordinary frock. It was the sort owned by rich girls and princesses. All that year I wore it to birthday parties and whenever people admired it I told them it was given to me by my father.

Anyone could tell he was a special person. He'd served in the army. He was called Captain, unlike my friends' fathers who were all plain Misters. Grandma and Grandpa had broad Yorkshire accents like mine, but my daddy's voice was posh like the newsreader on the BBC. He wore a bowler hat and carried a black umbrella, and my grandmother told me he lived in London where our Queen had her palace.

Saturday morning, my mother rose early and went into town to buy a joint of beef, leaving me to make the horseradish sauce. I dug up the root, washed it and then rubbed it against the grater. At once my eyes began to smart and even though I was happy about my father's visit, I couldn't help crying.

At twelve o'clock a shiny black car pulled up in front of the house. My mother galloped down the back steps and ran up the path to the gate. We all hugged, and my father allowed me to carry his bag into the house. Grandpa and Grandma were at the door to greet him and everyone had a wonderful afternoon.

That night I had to sleep in the camping bed with the metal springs that creaked and dug into me when I turned over. My mother set it at the foot of the big bed we normally shared. Before I went to sleep she heard me say my prayers – first the Lord's, and then the 'God bless Daddy and Mummy' one that ended with 'and may we soon have our own little house and all live together again.' Then she tucked me in and reminded me it was nearly Easter.

There was a gap between the curtains that let in the morning light and woke me early. The window seemed to be in the wrong place and for a moment I couldn't think where I was. Then I heard the sound of heavy breathing and remembered I had slept in the camp bed, and my father was lying beside my mother.

The high bed end hid me from my parents, but I felt uncomfortable – embarrassed. I gathered my clothes and was careful not to look towards the bed as I tiptoed out the door and went to dress in the bathroom.

When everyone was awake I was given my chocolate egg. But there was no time to eat it for we were all off to church, where my mother walked down the aisle on my father's arm, smiling at the congregation and looking for all the world like a bride.

And then, before I could introduce him to my new cat, Timmy, or show him how good I'd become at drawing butterflies and ponies, my father was saying goodbye and telling me to be a good girl for my mother. And I knew it would be a long time before I saw him again.

Neighbours

My grandparents and their neighbours built their houses at the same time, shortly before the start of the First World War. They remained in them ever after, living close enough to be familiar with each other's ways, and a party to family secrets. And yet in all those years they rarely entered one another's homes.

Instead the women met on the street. They whispered of sickness or scandal while the fishmonger weighed out haddock and cod. On Tuesdays they chatted in the mobile library while exchanging their books, and on Thursdays when the greengrocer rang his bell, they hurried out to gossip beside his cart. That too, was the signal for my grandfather to rush to the front gate with his shovel, ready to scoop up horse manure to put on his roses.

But as my grandmother's regular messenger, I was familiar with the insides of all their homes. It was my job to deliver jars of newly made jam to Mrs Oliver and to send for Mrs Spurr, the butcher's wife, when someone was sick. She knew what to do. She was good with animals too, although she couldn't save my pet rabbit when he ate pyrethrum daisies.

I liked Mrs Riggs the best. After I'd delivered my grandmother's messages we walked together in her garden, where the scent of lilac mingled with lavender and mock orange. Before I left she always went to a cupboard in the kitchen and brought out a box of handmade chocolates, so exquisite that choosing was nigh impossible. When I finally picked one out she slipped another into my pocket.

A small, particular sort of person, she was neatly dressed whatever the time of my visit. She did have that bit of trouble though when she was holidaying in Morecambe with Mr Riggs.

On their first evening they went for a walk along the pier. After a while Mrs Riggs grew tired and suggested they return to the guesthouse, but her husband grumbled because he was enjoying his stroll. Mrs Riggs, who had missed her usual afternoon tea, urged him to get a move on, and when he took no notice and continued to meander along, she grew irritated and decided to walk on alone.

She'd almost reached the guesthouse when she remembered her husband had the key to their room. She would have to go back and look for him.

As it happened, he wasn't far away. Mr Riggs was still making no attempt to hurry. Indeed, he'd stopped again and was leaning over the railings, gazing out to sea. Fuming, Mrs Riggs marched over to him and with her open hand, delivered him a hearty whack across the buttocks. Mr Riggs spun around, mouth wide open in shock.

Only it wasn't Mr Riggs. It was a man Mrs Riggs had never set eyes on before.

The beck

Beyond the back fence of The Limes, a meadow sloped down to the beck, a gently flowing stream of bright water where blue-green dragonflies hovered above golden kingcups.

At the start of the summer holiday my grandfather made nets by wiring flour bags onto garden canes, and when my best friend Pauline came to play we fished for red-throated sticklebacks in the stream. If we were lucky and caught one we took it home in a jam jar to show my mother, before setting it free again.

Watercress grew there in clumps and we took that home to her too, after first shaking off the button-like snails that clung to its roots. She was glad of it and added it to Marmite in our brown-bread sandwiches.

We didn't always take off our shoes and often used the beck's green islands as stepping stones. That wasn't without risk, and once in a while one of us arrived home with a dirty white sock and a shoe caked in mud. But as long as we turned up for lunch, our mothers allowed us to climb trees, wander down lanes, and set off on long treks together.

Once we climbed over a wall into a field where cornflowers and scarlet poppies bobbed their heads among the barley. In the centre was a ruined cottage. Vines of deadly nightshade ran over its walls, and to us it seemed an exciting and dangerous place to play.

As far as I was concerned the meadow at the bottom of my garden was ours – Pauline's and mine – our own private playground. The farmer who owned it knew us well, because we bounced on his haystacks and helped him feed spare milk to the stray cats that hung around his dairy. He didn't mind us at all.

We both wanted to ride and wished the farmer had horses as well as cows. There was a fallen tree lying near the beck and on its branches, with the help of hair ribbons and painted eyes, we galloped far and wide.

In the springtime a bevy of pink-tongued calves with steaming breath grazed and gambolled in our field. We picked bunches of the richest grass we could find and held it out to them. One by one they lost their shyness, trotted over to be fed and stood in a tight circle around us.

When my grass was all gone I tried to move away, but I hadn't noticed the hungry calf chewing my skirt. I tugged the material out of her mouth, but it was scrunched up and shiny with cow slaver, and I knew my mother wouldn't be pleased.

A footpath crossed the field from a gate at the bottom to a stile at the top beside our back fence. Grandpa said it was an ancient 'right of way', which meant walkers could use it whenever they wished.

Now and then the farmer allowed his bull to run with the cows. I played in that field every day. I knew where the thrushes and blackbirds nested. I knew when the first buttercups and daisies were coming into flower, and where to find fish in the beck. And I knew when the bull was in the field.

Those who crossed it obviously did not.

I watched from a secret place by the fence as young couples or groups of friends slowly wound their way up the hill towards me. They must have seen the cows peacefully chewing away on their cud, but I knew they hadn't noticed the bull lurking in their midst.

The singing class

Except for John Mellor who said I was fat and called me Sally Sausage, I liked all the children in my class. I was fond of our teacher too. Whether we had a sore tummy, a bruised knee or just wanted to go home to our mummies, Miss Fretwell pressed us against her soft bosoms, wiped away our tears and made us happy again.

She taught us to count and measure, to read and to write the alphabet. On sunny afternoons she led us out to the school meadow where bumblebees droned in the wildflowers, and read us stories while we threaded daisy chains and hung them around our necks.

One morning Miss Fretwell said, 'Today you're going to have a music lesson.'

Forty-two of us lined up in pairs ready to march into the school hall, and I held hands with Pauline because she was my best friend. A lady was waiting for us. She said her name was Miss Ponsonby. She didn't smile and I didn't like the way her eyes bulged like a goldfish's.

She began the lesson by playing a tune on the piano while we la-la-d. After that she clapped out the beat of 'What shall we do with the drunken sailor?' and had us repeat the words until we knew them by heart. I was just beginning to enjoy myself when Maureen, a shy girl with a birthmark on her cheek, put up her hand and asked if she could go to the toilet.

'No you may not!' yelled Miss Ponsonby, smashing her hand down on the piano and making us all jump.

Miss Fretwell always let us to go if we asked. She'd even allow us to take a friend along. We sat up, straight as pokers, giving each other frightened looks.

The new teacher started to play the next piece, but in a minute Maureen put up her hand again.

'Miss,' she said, with a tremble in her voice, 'I really need to go.'

'You'll have to wait,' said Miss Ponsonby. 'I won't have children trooping in and out of my lesson.' She glared at us. 'And that goes for all of you.'

We tried the song again but our previously lusty voices had shrunk to whispers. I was glad I'd visited the toilet block at playtime. But then I felt a little 'low-down' pressure. I needed to go too!

What if I weed on the floor? I'd seen a boy do that once. Miss Fretwell didn't make a fuss. She cleaned it up with the big mop and called his mother to tell her to bring in clean undies, but the whole class made fun of him. I squeezed my knees together and tried to think of something else. Just then the bell rang for lunch and I was able to run outside.

The next time Miss Fretwell announced that we should line up for singing, she seemed surprised by the sudden flurry of raised hands. There was a long queue outside the toilet and Pauline and I were at the end of it. After it was our turn, we washed our hands with a slab of brown soap, working up a lather and putting off the moment when we'd have to face the fierce new teacher again.

By the time we'd emerged from the toilet block the playground was deserted and we could hear singing coming from the hall. We rushed inside and slipped down among the children in the back row.

'Stand up, you two!' boomed Miss Ponsonby. 'How dare you be late.'

Grasping our arms, she frog-marched us to the front of the class and dumped us on the floor at her feet. Then she clapped out the rhythm of another song and seemed to forget about us, but I was shaking with fear and daren't so much as glance at Pauline.

Miss Ponsonby strode up and down in front of us, her tweed skirt swirling around her calves while she demonstrated how we should puff up our chests to force out the high notes. We copied her until, satisfied with our efforts, she turned back to the piano.

At that instant there was a little twanging sound, just loud enough to be heard by those of us in the front row, and a sugar-pink suspender dropped to the floor at Miss Ponsonby's feet. We watched transfixed as she bent down and scooped it up with only the slightest break in her stride. Then she plopped down onto the piano stool and hid her face behind her music book.

It was too late. We'd all seen the flush of embarrassment on her cheeks. It would have been more than our lives were worth to giggle, but I sneaked a glance at my friends and could tell everyone was secretly delighted.

After that, singing lessons no longer frightened me, and I didn't need to go to the toilet before I went into the hall. And over the following years Miss Ponsonby taught me some memorable songs that have stayed with me all of my life.

Bluebells

Sometimes on warm clear days, my mother cut cucumber sandwiches and packed them in her shopping bag, together with hard-boiled eggs and two of Grandpa's apples, in preparation for a picnic.

We walked down to the bottom of the hill and along Common Lane, between hedgerows bursting with the spicy-sweet scent of hawthorn. Then we followed the railway tracks until we came to an old iron footbridge, which we had to cross to reach the bluebell woods on the other side.

I hesitated. There was something scary about that bridge, so far from the village and leading to nowhere in particular. It gave me a creepy feeling, and as I climbed its steps I held tightly to my mother's hand. Through the gaps in the floor I could see the railway tracks far below and I was afraid I might fall.

But once we were safely on the other side I knew it was all worthwhile, for beneath the elms and beeches I saw a sapphire lake of bluebells, its surface shifting and rippling in the wind.

Market day

It was Friday, market day, and a bitterly cold morning for shopping. I pressed close to my mother's arm in the plastic smell of her umbrella, as bullets of hail exploded onto the pavement around us.

My mother glanced down at her watch and I could feel her body tense. 'Your father told me he'd ring at one,' she said. 'I don't want to miss him.'

The stallholder sliced into a wheel of Wensleydale, the cheese falling off the wire in soft white crumbs.

'How much?' my mother asked, fumbling in her purse. She counted out the right change and had it in the man's hand even before he could pass her the cheese. Then she set off for the bus station at such a pace that I struggled to keep up.

'I was going to look for a cotton off-cut to make you a blouse,' she said between breaths. 'We'll have to do that another day.'

The double-decker bus was standing in its bay, empty apart from a boy in Scout uniform and the woman conductor waiting on the step. We climbed aboard and sat down. My mother looked at her watch again and then leant across me and peered through the window, searching for the driver. When he emerged from the tearoom she breathed a sigh of relief.

But he drifted slowly across the bus station, stopping along the way to chat with the other drivers. When he reached our bus he walked around the back and started talking to the conductor. Minutes slipped away. My mother shifted around in her seat. At last the driver climbed into his cab, the bell rang and the bus set off with a jerk.

Back home, Grandma was sitting at the table shelling peas. She looked up, startled, when my mother burst into the kitchen.

'Has he rung?'

'Not yet.'

No peace until he did.

A meeting in London

I showed my mother the note but I didn't expect to go because I knew we couldn't afford expensive overseas holidays. All the same, she read the letter twice. Then she went to the cupboard and brought out her old red moneybox.

'We'll put in a little bit every week,' she told me. 'We may have to do without a few things, and there'll be no more pocket money for you, but I'm determined. You're going on that trip.'

So somehow she scraped the money together, and I went to Switzerland with the Girl Guides and stayed in a village near Interlaken. I rode in a cable car and saw a glacier. I walked through meadows filled with alpine flowers, woke in the morning to the sound of cowbells, and learnt that Swiss ladies air their doonas by hanging them out of the window.

On the way home we stopped in London and saw the Palace and the Tower, and walked around the shops. A greengrocer's had all sorts of interesting vegetables I hadn't seen before, and I spent the last of my money on a round, green fruit. The man said it was a honeydew melon and that it was sweet and juicy. I found it would just fit into my rucksack if I didn't draw up the string.

There was to be a special ending to my trip – my father was coming to take me to dinner.

I hung around the door of the Youth Hostel peering out at the passing taxis, knowing he'd be in one of them. While I waited, I realised how little I remembered of the years before I was six, when we all lived together in London.

I knew that on my first day at school two big girls caught hold of my arms and made me eat a piece of chalk. I remembered Kensington Gardens: the sound of rustling leaves underfoot, the rabbits on Peter Pan's statue cool and smooth under my fingers, sailboats scudding across Round Pond.

I had a clear picture in my head of my mother dropping a shilling into a slot before she lit the gas fire in our flat. But of how it felt to live with my father, I remembered nothing at all.

A taxi pulled up and he beckoned. I hurried over and sat down on the back seat beside him.

'Aren't you going to give your daddy a kiss?' he asked.

I was embarrassed, shy. It had been more than a year since I last saw him. I leant over and planted a little one on his cheek. It was smooth. His hair was greased and slicked to one side, his tie neatly knotted. He was wearing an expensive-looking jacket and his bowler hat sat on his knee.

The taxi stopped in front of the Cumberland Hotel and we got out. I threw back my pigtails and followed the head waiter through the grand dining room to our table. The man pulled out my chair, waited until I was seated, and then opened my napkin and laid it on my knee. I felt like a princess.

My father picked up a menu, a book with gold binding, and asked me what I'd like to eat.

I thought for a moment and said, 'I'll have whatever you're having.'

Then I looked down at the rows of knives and forks beside my plate and suddenly felt stupid. When the first course arrived, four spears of asparagus in some sort of sauce, my father saw me hesitate.

He whispered, 'Use the ones on the outside first.'

There was a special knife for the fish that arrived next and another, serrated one, for the meat. Over dessert my father asked me about my holiday; whether I enjoyed being in the Girl Guides, how I was doing at school. He was charming and I had a wonderful time.

I'd have liked to ask him when I'd see him again and whether he'd visit us in Yorkshire soon – but I daren't.

FISH AND CHIPS

Hats

My mother's hats fill the middle shelf of the mahogany wardrobe, nestled inside one another like a row of birds' nests. Hats are her weakness and her way of coping when hope fades. At those times she leaves me with my grandmother, pulls on her old blue mackintosh and takes the bus into town. An hour or so later she reappears, refreshed, a bright smile on her lips.

'What do you think?' she asks, pirouetting around the kitchen so Grandma and I can view the new hat from every angle. No matter that it looks like a pork pie or a seagull in flight. 'It flatters your face. It makes you look younger. It matches the colour of your new winter coat,' we say, grateful for the remarkable lift in her mood.

Fish and chips

It's often a year or more between my father's visits, yet all through primary school I wait patiently for him to come and take us away. And there's never a day when he doesn't call to reassure my mother that we'll soon be living together again as a normal family.

But then I turn twelve and win a scholarship to the Girls' High School and everything changes. My old friend, Pauline, goes off to a different school and I rarely get to see her. Instead I make friends with the daughters of doctors and dentists and stockbrokers, and they invite me into their homes. I meet their parents, who soon ask me about mine.

'Does your father play golf? What does he do for a living?'

What *does* he do for a living? I have no idea. I can't even tell them where he lives. On the rare occasions my mother goes to London to see him, he meets her on the platform at King's Cross station. He takes her to lunch at Lyons Corner House and afterwards for a walk in the park. Then he sees her back onto the train.

'Does he live in London?' I ask her. 'Or does he travel there from somewhere else?'

She doesn't know.

'Why don't you get him to tell you where he lives?'

She hedges. Although my father phones every day, in all these years he hasn't given her his telephone number.

One night after his usual call, she tells me excitedly, 'I heard a clock chime in the background. It made me think he was in a living room.' She says she's relieved because she'd begun to suspect he was in prison and hadn't wanted to tell us.

Often there's talk of money – lots of it. Money temporarily tied up by accountants and lawyers.

'Once it comes through, your father's going to buy us a big, beautiful house,' my mother says. And on another occasion, 'He's buying your grandfather a car. It'll be here any day now.'

Grandpa's excited and keeps asking about his new Rover. After a while though, I can tell he's beginning to doubt it will ever appear. The next time my father calls, my grandfather races up the hallway, passing my mother on the way and beating her to the phone. I hear him loudly demanding to know what's going on. But as my mother always says, 'Your father could charm the birds out of the trees,' and Grandpa comes away convinced his car will arrive eventually. All the same, I can tell he's tired of my father's stories.

Then one evening my mother comes out of the telephone room and tells us to expect a visit. Now, I think, there'll be a fight and my grandfather will finally get to the bottom of all this. But when my father arrives there is no argument, and I watch Grandpa usher him into the back room, sit him down in an armchair and pour him a glass of his best whisky. Like the little boy in the story of *The Emperor's New Clothes*, I'm the only one to see through the fantasy. And that makes me feel lonely.

At times my mother still calls out, 'Sally! Be quick! Your father wants to speak to you.'

When I was younger I rushed to the phone and thrilled at the sound of his voice. 'How are you, my dear? Are you doing well at school?'

'Yes I am, Daddy,' I'd say.

Then he'd tell me to put my mother back on.

I don't do that anymore. Nowadays when I hear my mother call out I hide behind the front room door. She knows I don't want to speak to my father but if she sees me she'll insist on my going to the phone.

'It's not for you to decide whether you want to talk to him,' Grandma says. 'It doesn't matter what he has or hasn't done, he's still your father.'

I wish he wasn't. He's become my guilty secret; the one that must be hidden from neighbours and friends, the reason I'm different and somehow inferior to the other girls I know. I resolve that in future when my friends ask me about my father, I'll say he lives in London, and I'll hint at a divorce.

My mother makes the best fish and chips in Yorkshire. Her brittle, golden batter coats thick slabs of haddock and cod that break into juicy white flakes. Her chips, made from freshly peeled potatoes and fried in lard, are wonderfully crisp on the outside and creamy in the middle.

Four days a week I eat lunch at school where gristly lumps of beef float in seas of insipid gravy, and mashed potato is peppered with 'eyes' that have missed the cook's knife. But as a treat, on Tuesdays, I come home for fish and chips.

'I'd like to meet your friends,' Mother says one day. 'Why don't you bring them with you next time?'

That sounds like fun, and the following week three girls from my class join me for lunch. My mother has just fried up a second basket of chips and we're sitting around the kitchen table tucking into them, when the phone rings and she jumps up. There's so much chatter and laughter I don't notice her return. But she wants us all to hear about the telephone call.

'That was your father,' she announces with pride in her voice. 'He's coming next week and he's promised to go with me to your school speech day.'

I look around at my friends' faces. I see surprise, and then curiosity – and I flush with embarrassment and shame.

Dirk and Dave

Ever since I started secondary school I've been madly, passionately, unable-to-sleep-for-thinking-about-him, in love. Perhaps it's the way his top lip curves upwards at one corner, making him appear a little standoffish and vulnerable. More likely it's the hint of sadness in his dark eyes that turns my legs to jelly. My mother has a saying, 'Still waters run deep,' and that describes him perfectly – a calm surface concealing an undercurrent of passion.

I long to feel his arms around me, to have his lips touch mine, and I dream of our future life together. But it is not to be. The letters I write him remain unanswered. He doesn't know of my existence, even though I've joined his fan club. And when, in *A Tale of Two Cities*, Dirk Bogarde walks to the guillotine, I think that I too will die.

Then one morning as I'm standing in the queue at the bus stop waiting to go to school, a young man glances in my direction. My heart leaps. He has Dirk's eyes! Those same dark pools with their hidden depths. I wait until he turns away and then I sneak a good long look at him. He's wearing the uniform of the Boys' Grammar, a school a few blocks from mine. He's catching my bus so he must live nearby. But who is he?

The bus arrives and we get on. I follow him inside, where he takes the last free seat. I'll happily stand all the way into town just to be near him, but the conductor catches my arm.

'Plenty of seats upstairs, luv,' he says.

With a reluctant glance over my shoulder I climb the steps to the top deck. When we reach the bus station I jump up, hoping to see the boy again, but a man who was sitting at the back is already on the stairs. He's short of breath and he's taking them one at a time. When I finally get to the bottom my Dirk Bogarde look-alike has gone.

At teatime I casually mention to my grandmother that there was a stranger on the bus. Does she know of a new family moving into our street?

She hasn't heard of one.

That night I lie awake trying to imagine myself going on a date with the boy with the beautiful eyes. But then I have a terrible thought. What if I never see him again?

I'm normally a slow starter in the mornings, leaving it until the last minute to get dressed and pack my schoolbag, but even if the bus is due, my mother refuses to let me leave until I've eaten something. Often that means standing by the gate with a cup of tea in one hand and a piece of toast in the other. I keep a sharp eye on the bottom of the hill, and if I see the bus coming, there's just enough time to drop everything and race to the stop. But since I saw that boy I get up as soon as I hear the alarm, and I know my mother's wondering what's going on.

A few days pass before my new heart-throb reappears in the morning queue. He glances in my direction but it's as if he hasn't seen me. I'm not altogether surprised. I don't stand out in a crowd, especially in school uniform. The shapeless pinafore dress does nothing for my figure – not that I have one. My breasts, those tiny pink cones that stick out little more than an inch beyond my chest, are a constant disappointment. The only aspect of my appearance that might attract a man's attention is my long hair, but for school I have to wear it in a ponytail and the top forms a silly lump under my hateful navy-blue beret.

I live in hope. Perhaps one day I'll find myself alone with him at the bus stop and I'll be able to strike up a conversation. But I know I won't. I blush scarlet if a boy speaks to me and my armpits sweat so much that they leave telltale marks on my dress.

Another week passes without my seeing him. Was he staying with relatives and has now gone away? Then it strikes me. He's catching a later bus!

In the morning I say goodbye to my mother and go down to the stop as usual, but when the bus comes I let it go and wait for the next. I figure that if I run all the way up Kirkgate I'll make it to school just in time for the bell.

Sure enough, as the second bus pulls up, my love emerges from a gate a few yards from where I'm standing and hops onto the platform. I get to sit next to him all the way into town! Our legs almost touch and once, when he pulls out a book and starts doing his homework, his hand brushes against mine.

I decide to tell my friend Jane about my so-far-unrequited love and ask her advice. 'I wanted to speak to him, but I couldn't think of anything to say.'

'Why don't you ask him to take you to the pictures?'

'But I don't even know his name.'

'I'll find out who he is,' says Jane after I describe him in detail. 'I know quite a few of the boys at the Grammar.'

We're sitting in the biology lab a few days later when she whispers, 'His name is David, and he's the friend of a boy I know. Tell you what, it's my birthday in a fortnight and I'm having a party. I'll invite him. You can dress up in your finery and I'll introduce you.'

I could hug her. No longer will I lie in bed at night dreaming of a love that can never be. When David sees me in my new dress and with my hair let down, he'll fall for me and I'll have a real boyfriend at last.

Before leaving for the party I spend an hour in front of the mirror combing my hair this way and that. A nasty little pimple has erupted between my nose and my top lip but my mother, whom now knows about my future boyfriend, helps me hide it under foundation cream. Wearing the white broderie anglaise dress with a pink satin bow that she has made for the occasion, I feel unusually confident.

As promised, when I arrive at her house, Jane introduces me to David and to another boy who's come to the party with him. She turns up the music and before I know it, we're all four dancing together and David has his arm around my waist. I'm in heaven.

Then the tempo of the music slows. Jane and David pair off, leaving me to dance with his friend. Hopefully I'll soon have another chance to spend time alone with David. But when the record ends he walks Jane to the couch, where they sit with their heads together and repeatedly burst into peals of laughter. How could she?

She knows how I feel about him. She's supposed to be my friend.

After a while the two get up and come over to where I'm stuck with this boy who is friendly enough, but doesn't have David's beautiful brown eyes.

'How about going to the pictures together?' asks Dave. 'A double date?'

I know what he means of course. Him and Jane – his friend and me. I'm about to say, 'No thanks,' when it strikes me that I've never been asked out on a date and this might be my only chance. So I change my mind, and surprisingly have a good time.

And so after going steady for the next three years we become engaged and I end up marrying that pleasant-looking boy with the ordinary blue eyes.

The bus to Leeds

The upstairs of the double-decker bus is filled with chattering mill girls heading to work on the late shift. Their heads are full of rollers tightly secured under net scarves. And that's where they'll stay until the weekend when the hair will be unwound and bouffanted, ready for a night on the town.

I gaze out the window at nothing in particular, only half hearing the girls' gossip, for within my heart I feel a little frisson of excitement. It's five months since my fifteenth birthday and I'm going on a date with my boyfriend.

In a few minutes we reach the Chantry Bridge, where the fourteenth-century chapel contrasts starkly with the grime-covered woollen mills

that surround it. At once the bus drives into a snowstorm, as gusts of wind whip up drifting soap suds from the river's surface and blow them across the road.

We enter Westgate and come to a halt. The mill girls clatter down the stairs and disappear into the gathering darkness. The conductor rings the bell, the bus gives a lurch and we rattle off along the road to Leeds. I've visited the city with my mother but I'm only familiar with the main shopping area, so my boyfriend is meeting me at the bus station.

Ten minutes out of Wakefield we run into fog. It's a common occurrence in November, especially after Guy Fawkes Night when it's triggered by smoke from all the bonfires. It envelops the bus in a heavy yellow blanket and I breathe in the smog's rank smell of dissolved chemicals.

In a few minutes night falls. I peer through the window but can no longer make out the streetlights. It's bitterly cold on top of the bus, and my gloves and scarf don't stop my shivering.

Periodically the bell rings as another passenger reaches his or her destination. Two young people sit behind me but soon they disappear down the stairs. Now I'm alone, apart from a man sitting two rows ahead on the other side of the bus.

He's black – shiny, ebony black. I study him surreptitiously. I've never been close to a black man before, or known anyone who wasn't typically 'English'. The residents of Walton are all white and Yorkshire-born like me. When my Aunt Pam returned from overseas with an Italian fiancé he was the talk of the village: how tanned he was, how he looked like Rossano Brazzi, the star of *South Pacific*. But the nearest I've come to seeing a dark-skinned person was when my Sunday school teacher showed us pictures of missionaries helping poor little black children in Africa.

I am familiar with the word 'nigger'. It's written on the lid of the brown polish my mother uses on her shoes. And I've repeated it since I was little, in a song my friends and I chanted parrot-fashion in a game at primary school. But it was simply a rhyming word that had no meaning.

Once I asked my grandfather whether black people were like us. He didn't answer directly, but I was left with the impression that they weren't as smart as white people and might possibly be a bit dangerous.

I consider my companion carefully.

The bus slows to a crawl. Obviously the driver is struggling to keep to the road in the decreasing visibility. I look at my watch and am disappointed to see that I'm already late, so late that we'll miss the show at the cinema.

The bus jerks to an abrupt halt and the driver calls out, 'Everybody off!'

I stand up, clamber down the winding staircase and step into the night. The smog is so thick I can't see my own feet.

'Where are we?' I ask the conductor.

He shrugs. 'Somewhere in Hunslet.'

'How am I going to get to the bus station?'

'Well, this bus isn't going any farther. It's too dangerous. You'll just have to walk.' He goes off to talk to the driver.

I've no idea where I am, or how I'm going to reach the middle of the city. I do know something about Hunslet though. It's a rundown area with a reputation for poverty and crime. It's no place for a young woman at night.

I check the bottom section of the bus for other passengers, but it's deserted. Hearing a clatter behind me, I turn around in time to see the black man from upstairs step off the bus. Terrified of being left alone in the darkness, I rush over and catch hold of his arm before he can disappear.

'Please, can you help? I don't know how to get to the bus station.'

'Come with me,' he says.

After a moment's hesitation I let him take my hand, and he leads me off into the night.

The shops and houses are vague, huddled shapes and I marvel at the man's ability to find his way. He doesn't speak to me again and I'm too shy and nervous to talk to him. It's some time before we see the first lights. Soon after, we emerge onto a wide street with brightly lit shop windows, and in a few minutes we arrive at the bus station where my boyfriend is waiting.

'Thank you,' I say. 'I was lucky to find someone who was coming into town too.'

The man shakes his head. 'No, I live in Hunslet. I'll go home now.'

He crosses the street and disappears into the fog.

Delia

She was my friend. Not my best friend, just a girl I knew. We were both members of a select little group of would-be artists who met in the craft room on Tuesday mornings. We sat at the same table and often sought each other's advice about our work. I drew street scenes, a fine pen for the buildings followed by a few sepia washes. Delia was experimenting with coloured inks too, but her pictures were bolder and brighter than mine.

Once in a while we sneaked out of school together to view the latest exhibition of abstract painting in the art gallery over the road. But we didn't visit each other's houses or meet regularly after school. That would have been difficult even if we'd wanted to, since she lived some distance away in a village with a poor bus service. It wasn't much of a place – a few hundred people, a railway line without a station, and no pub. Her father was headmaster of the local primary school, a well-respected man and a deacon of the church.

She was shorter than me and daintily built, had a neat head of mouse-brown hair and a look of being quietly self-possessed. Unlike some girls I knew, she didn't hitch her skirts above her knees or flirt with the boys from the Grammar on her way down to the bus station. And she never mentioned a boyfriend. She was a quiet, well-brought-up sort of girl.

I think that like me, she was a little afraid of our teachers: their enforcement of absolute silence in the corridors, the insistence on ladylike behaviour at all times, the shaming in school assembly of any girl who dared take off her beret before reaching home.

Delia was no troublemaker and since she wasn't musical, exceptional at sport or unusually clever, she probably would have passed through school almost unnoticed if it hadn't been for what happened later.

That week I brought a painting of my cat to school to show her. I thought she'd like it, but when I looked around I realised she was missing from class. At first I assumed she was sick, but then the rumours started and it wasn't long before I was reading about her in the newspaper.

It said Delia's boyfriend had already turned sixteen, so was a year older than her; that they were neighbours and had been childhood friends. Apparently she'd told her mother first, and then accompanied her to the doctor to have it confirmed. I imagine she would have wanted to be certain before she broke the news to her father. In the end I don't know if she ever did tell him, for that same evening the couple walked hand in hand into the railway tunnel at the edge of the village and waited for the train.

The engine driver never stood a chance. The pair couldn't have been more than a few yards away when he spotted them, or perhaps in the darkness he never saw them at all. They found Delia's body in the tunnel. The train had pushed the boy's along the tracks and out into the fading sunlight.

Our headmistress mentioned the 'unfortunate incident earlier in the week' during assembly, and insisted we girls not discuss the matter in school. She said nothing of Delia herself; the funny little stories she told, how beautifully she painted. And when two of my classmates tried to talk about her to our home teacher, they were immediately silenced.

We were only fifteen. For many of us it was the first time we'd been touched by death. We walked around with handkerchiefs against our faces and cried in dark corners.

One afternoon I overheard my mother's friends talking. They seemed unable to comprehend why two children would want to kill themselves. I didn't understand their surprise. Surely they were familiar with the phrase, 'A fate worse than death'?

In villages the size of Delia's, news spreads rapidly. It wouldn't have been long before everyone believed that her father, that fine upstanding churchman, had raised a slut. And what of the school? How could she have faced our formidable headmistress and told her she was pregnant? I know I couldn't have.

I've wondered since why her boyfriend chose to die. He too would have had to weather his parents' anger, but their neighbours would have probably made allowances for his carelessness and put it down to bad luck. Perhaps he feared charges would be laid against him, since he'd turned sixteen and she wasn't of legal age.

But I believe he walked into the tunnel on that glorious summer evening because he loved Delia, he couldn't live without her, and he didn't want her to die alone.

The Sunday after her death I went to evensong, but only half-heard the service. I spent most of it gazing up at the stained-glass window above the altar, thinking about all that had happened. Our vicar was on holiday and a visiting priest gave the sermon.

'I know you've all heard about last week's tragedy in our neighbouring parish,' he began.

With a rustle, everyone straightened in their seats. Our vicar, a cold fish of a man, would never have mentioned such a shameful thing.

'Why was it,' our visitor continued, 'that two children, members of a church community, had no one to turn to in their hour of need?'

I glanced across at the ladies in their expensive hats and white-lace gloves, and at their well-to-do husbands, those pillars of the church – and I saw them squirm. Had *they* been approached they wouldn't have helped the troubled pair either. And they knew it.

The house in the village

We're washing up in the kitchen when there's a thump above our heads. My mother flies out of the room, but by the time she reaches the top of the stairs my grandfather is already lying dead on the floor. We know he's had bouts of angina, but it's a huge shock.

I'm slowly becoming accustomed to not having him around, but I miss him terribly. I can see him still: peeling an apple in an unbroken, curling ribbon, brushing my hair while I sit by the fireside, collecting leaves to make a winter bed for my tortoise. Cracking almonds in a vice and feeding them to me, one at a time. And I never walk in his garden without thinking of him.

Since his passing we've gone on living together at The Limes, my mother, my grandmother and I, though with luck I'll be leaving for college in a couple of years.

Grandma's in her eighties, has arthritis in both knees and spends much of her time in bed. That's hard on my mother who is forever running up and down stairs, and she's growing older too. If only for her sake, my grandmother would like to part with the big house and move into a smaller place, preferably with all the rooms on the same level.

There's a problem. Even though she was married to my grandfather for fifty years she can't sell The Limes because her name isn't on the deeds. According to the terms of Grandpa's will, she's allowed to stay on until she dies, but then the house must pass to my auntie. She will sell it – and my mother will be homeless.

I think my grandmother should be free to do whatever she wants with her house, but at the same time I can understand my grandfather's reasoning. My aunt's a widow, she's not well off and she has a young daughter. For all these years my mother has insisted that her husband is going to buy us a big, beautiful home. Perhaps Grandpa believed her, or more likely, thought that by writing his will like that he'd force my father to provide for her. Either way, it's a serious problem and hardly a day passes without my mother mentioning it to me, saying how afraid she is for her future.

I lie awake at night wondering what I can do to help. It's high time she found out more about my father: where he lives, whether there's any truth in his stories about coming into money. At least then she'd know what to expect from him, and could make realistic plans for the time when my grandmother is no longer with us.

Aware that I know next to nothing about him myself, I decide to take the train to London and visit Somerset House where records of births, deaths and marriages are stored, to see what I can find out. Before I leave I ask my mother to tell me anything that might help me with my search.

She talks fleetingly about my father's family, telling me my grandfather on that side is long gone, and mentioning an uncle who emigrated to Rotorua, in New Zealand. My father is sixteen years older than my mother and was already into his forties when they married. I know he's a real charmer and obviously likes the opposite sex.

'Did he ever mention anyone else?' I ask. 'Or an earlier marriage?'

Her face clouds over. 'Just once, he spoke of a Spanish woman,' she says, 'but I don't think he married her.'

She talks at length of a time before I was born, when my father was an officer in the army. They lived together in London during the Blitz, and later on the Isle of Tiree in the Outer Hebrides, where he was in command of a unit. I can tell from the warmth in her voice when she speaks of her life on the island that those were her golden days. But overall, the information she provides doesn't give me much to go on.

It costs money to look at records and I need to be careful to order the right ones. I begin with my birth certificate. Both my parents' names appear on it. Next I ask to see their marriage certificate. I notice it's dated three months after my birth. Why? They'd already been living together for years. If they were concerned about my being illegitimate, why didn't they wed as soon as my mother found out she was pregnant? Or else not bother at all?

I'd like to find out more about my father but with one of the commonest surnames in all England and so little information, my quest appears hopeless.

I return home and try talking to my mother again, but her answers are vague and she soon changes the subject. It's then I think of the Salvation Army and a scheme I've read of, in which missing family members are traced. I tell my mother about it and promise to find out where my father lives. She seems excited by the idea, and I go to bed determined to contact the Army in the morning.

Next day I'm eating my cornflakes when she joins me in the kitchen. She looks worried. 'I've thought it over,' she says. 'You mustn't do that. You mustn't try to find your father. He'll find out we've been looking for him and he'll be angry.'

I'm angry. But I can't persuade her to let me go on with my search.

Over the next two years my grandmother's health steadily deteriorates, and I can tell she's becoming more and more worried about what will happen to my mother when she dies. Then just as I'm about to go off to college, she has an idea. She'll use what money she has left to buy a bungalow, and she'll rent out The Limes.

There's a small, two-bedroom place for sale in the village. It's brand new and sounds perfect. They go to look at it and it's not long before my grandmother puts down a deposit.

I'm overjoyed. I don't have to worry about my mother any more. The bungalow will be hers when Grandma finally passes away. She won't have to rely on my father's promises. Her future will be secure.

Everything goes according to plan. Shortly before the sale is finalised, my mother borrows a key and goes inside the house to measure up for the curtains. She finds some pretty, inexpensive chintz in the market and sets about making them herself.

She's sitting at the old treadle sewing machine in the kitchen finishing off a hem, when the phone rings and she jumps up to answer it. My grandmother gives me a tired look. We know who it is. On this occasion my mother's away longer than usual, and when she returns her cheeks are flushed.

'That was your father,' she says. 'I decided to tell him about the bungalow. And do you know what? He said it wasn't good enough, that I shouldn't have to live in a housing estate at the wrong end of the village. He says his money's coming through shortly and he's promised, absolutely promised, that in less than a month he'll buy me a better place in a much nicer area.'

'He's been talking about buying a house since I was a little girl,' I tell her. 'Surely you don't believe him?' Then conscious of a bad feeling in the pit of my stomach I add, 'You are still going through with it, aren't you? You're moving into the bungalow?'

But she isn't. And my grandmother loses her deposit.

Teachers' college

I cross the lawn, enter the main building and make my way to the principal's office. I've received a message that he wants to see me, but I can't think why. When I knock on his door he shows me into the oval room and we sit down in front of a magnificent bay window overlooking the lake.

By the way he fidgets in his chair, I can tell that whatever it is he has to discuss with me is making him uncomfortable. He asks a few general questions about how I've settled in and whether I'm enjoying my course.

Then he clears his throat and says, 'I invited you here so we could talk about your grant. There's a bit of a problem.'

I'm puzzled. As far as I know all the students at the college receive free tuition, food and accommodation. The government even provides a generous book allowance.

The principal, a stocky, broad-faced man, looks down at a piece of paper lying in his lap. 'This is your grant application. Your father has filled it in and declared his income.' He leans towards me with a look of disbelief. 'He earns more than I do,' he says, 'and I'm a college principal!'

I stare at him in amazement.

'Your father's so wealthy that you are one of the few students in this country who isn't entitled to a grant.'

'But that's crazy! He only sends my mother a few pounds each week. If we didn't live with my grandparents we'd be destitute.'

The principal looks startled. 'In that case, why don't you go and talk to someone at County Hall?' He writes down a phone number and hands it to me. 'Tell them about your circumstances. I'm sure they'll help you.'

Aware that this may be my only chance of finding out where my father is living, I ask, 'May I see the form?'

'I'm sorry, but that's confidential. I'm not allowed to show it to you.'

I walk back to my room, and it's only then I realise I'm shaking. I struggle to make sense of what I've been told. Is my father a wealthy man? It seems unlikely. But if he isn't, why would he lie? Surely he wouldn't deliberately stop me receiving a grant?'

After a few minutes my friend Christine returns from her French horn lesson, notices that I'm curled up on the bed and asks me what's wrong.

It's not easy for me to explain. Although I had friends when I was at school I avoided talking to them about my home life. But Christine is a kind, warm person, and I soon find myself telling her all about the grant and my father's mysterious behaviour.

'They'll throw me out for sure. My mother can't pay the fees and I don't have any money.' I start to cry. 'I love it here. It'll break my heart if I have to leave.'

Christine puts her arms around me and tells me to calm down.

'I thought my mother would be able to fill out the form,' I tell her, 'but she said my father had to do that. I was stuck. I couldn't send it on to him because I didn't have his address. But in the end he contacted the college himself and had a copy sent direct.'

'If your father really is rich, he can afford to pay your fees,' Christine says. 'And if he isn't, they'll have to give you a grant.' She encourages me to follow the principal's suggestion and talk over my problem with someone at County Hall.

It's a huge building, and as I walk down its dimly lit corridors in search of room twenty-six, I feel increasingly nervous. I'm going to have to tell my story to a stranger.

As it happens, the man I eventually speak to makes it easy for me. He's sympathetic and eager to help. 'How much does your father send your mother each week?'

'Five pounds.'

'Then there's a simple solution to this. Ask her to put that in a letter and explain how she is separated from your father, and I'll make sure you receive the full allowance.'

I'm overjoyed to hear that the problem can be so easily resolved. I thank the man and go straight home to tell my mother the good news.

'I can't do that,' she says at once. 'I won't have people thinking your father and I are separated.'

'Mum, no one will know. The form's completely confidential. And this is the only way I can get a grant.'

But she can't bring herself to write the letter.

I return to Bretton, devastated. I've never been happier than in these last weeks. I like the staff and the group of musicians, sculptors, potters and flamboyant drama students with whom I share my life. I've fallen in love with the mansion itself: its ornate ceilings and marble fireplaces, Pillar Hall, Camellia House, and even the wainscotting in the bedroom I share with my friends.

Where else could I hear Chopin being played in the early morning? And at what other college would I be allowed to sit all day by a lake, painting the trees' reflections on the water?

I attend my usual classes while I wait to hear when I'm to be thrown out. Then amazingly, my mother calls to say that my father has paid the first term's fees and I am to become a teacher after all.

It's much later that I discover the first instalment was all he ever paid, and although my mother won't say, I suspect it was my grandmother's money that put me through college.

Down the pit

My grandfather built a pair of bay-windowed, semi-detached houses, each with ample rooms, attics above, workshops and cellars below. Then he moved into one of them and sold the other.

Once in a while we see the man who bought it standing out the front, resting his arms on his gate. As she walks by, my mother says, 'Good day.'

He answers her, 'Good day to you.'

But that's the most I ever hear pass between my family and the one next door. When I ask my mother why, she has a simple explanation.

'Because he works at the colliery.'

The miners' cottages at the bottom of the hill are small, terraced affairs – two up, two down, with a shared toilet across the yard. To afford a house like his, he must have a senior position and may even be a manager. It makes no difference. He works at the pit.

So despite having grown up in a village with a colliery, I've never spoken to anyone who works there.

I've seen the grey mountains of slag and the trail of smoke from the chimney. As a child I patted the stocky little pit ponies, brought to the surface for the holidays to eat their fill in the meadow by the church hall. I've been woken by the clatter of the miners' wooden clogs as they came home from their shift. I've heard their coughing, and in the morning seen the globs of black spittle left behind on the pavement. But I've never been to the pit at the other end of the village.

The only time I see coal is when a man with a leather jerkin and blackened face tosses a sack of it into our coal shed. Or when I throw another lump onto the fire. So that's why, when I'm told there's to be a college excursion to a coalmine, I decide to sign up for it.

A week later we're crammed together in the cage – lights on our helmets, batteries at our waists. Someone flicks a switch and suddenly we're falling from an aeroplane without a parachute. Just when I think I'm going to die, there's a surge that feels as though we're going back up again, but actually means the cage is slowing down. With a thump we reach the pit bottom and the door opens.

I expect to see the miners working in dark tunnels, but instead find myself standing in a towering cathedral with white-painted walls. We board a 'paddy' train that will take us to the coalface.

When it stops we turn on our helmet lights and walk into a tunnel. Gusts of wind from the ventilation shriek past our heads. Now and then we stumble over the rough ground as the roof gets lower and lower.

Our guide halts for a moment to speak to three men eating their lunch while squatting on a pile of coal. I'm shocked to see they've switched off their lights, presumably to conserve the batteries, and are eating their meal in total darkness amid the dust and filth.

We worm our way farther along the tunnel and then crawl between the hydraulic pit props in order to reach the coalface. There's a deafening row coming from the conveyer belt and the cutter. A cloud of black dust fills our noses and crusts around our eyes. It's hot, and here the miners are stripped to the waist and glisten with sweat. When they stop to rest there's just enough space for them to crouch with their heads close to their knees.

Without warning the self-advancing pit props move forward to keep pace with the cutter, at the same time allowing the roof to cave in behind them. It's unnerving – downright frightening. I'm relieved when our guide signals that it's time to leave. We return to the cage, and soon I'm back on the surface taking off my battery and hanging up my helmet.

I have finally met the miners whose dirty, dangerous work allows my family to have electric light, hot water, and a warm house all through winter.

The wedding

'Have you spoken to Uncle Jack yet?' I ask my mother, three weeks before the wedding.

'Yes I have.'

'And he'll give me away, as we agreed?'

'It should be your father who gives you away.'

'But we've already talked about this. He can come to the wedding if he wants, but not to be a part of it. We both know he's never been a father to me.'

Over the following hours I continue to plead with her but she's determined. My father must give me away.

He isn't contributing to the wedding. What money we've been able to scrape together has mostly come from my stints of holiday work at a chemist and a mail order firm. It would have been sufficient for the modest affair I first envisaged. But my in-laws would like to invite a lot of people and have the reception at the Fox and Hounds, an up-market place where the huntsmen meet in their red livery.

We've finally agreed that my mother and I will pay what we can afford and my future father-in-law will be responsible for the extras. It sounds reasonable, but I know that the bride's father is supposed to pay for everything, and I'd rather have stuck with the simpler occasion we originally planned.

I've organised the flowers, I've checked with the caterers, the bridesmaids have been to the dressmaker for their final fittings and my wedding dress is waiting in the wardrobe. In the daytime I look forward to marrying my childhood sweetheart, but at night I can't sleep for thinking of how it will feel to walk down the aisle on my father's arm.

Of course my mother has known all along that she'll have her way. Her only concession has been that Uncle Jack be allowed to make a speech and propose the toast to the bride and groom. Even she has to admit my father would be lost for words. What could he say about me? We haven't had a conversation in years.

He arrives the night before the wedding and insists on a kiss. I manage it somehow. It's not hate I feel. It's revulsion. My mother and grandmother make a great fuss of him but I do my best to keep out of his way.

In the morning it's sunny, a perfect day for a wedding. Christine, who is one of my bridesmaids, helps me into my dress. That's when I discover it no longer fits. I've lost so much weight in the last fortnight that it's hanging on me.

We congregate in Grandpa's garden and pose on the lawn for the photographer. There's a brief interlude of panic when a bee gets caught in my veil, but I manage to free it without being stung, and in a few minutes the Rolls arrives and we set off for the church. My father sits beside me on the back seat, but there's so much dress and veil between us that I don't have to look at him.

We arrive at the church, and the moment approaches when we will have to leave the dimly lit sanctuary of the porch and step forward into the aisle. Then everyone will turn around to gape at the strange man my mother talks of constantly, and who only appears at weddings and funerals.

DUCKS AND ROSES

Carr Lane Farm

After a honeymoon in Liechtenstein we move into our first home, a rambling farmhouse in Lancashire. Built in 1660, it has two staircases, huge rooms almost impossible to heat, and cavity stone walls wherein the mice run free. A new overflow town for Liverpool will eventually claim the surrounding land that is, in the meantime, given over to potatoes.

The house is a mile from the main road and the nearest bus stop. As I trudge home with a heavy bag of schoolbooks after a long day's teaching, I find myself wishing we could afford a second car. Instead my husband buys me a bike.

I haven't owned, or even ridden one before. But he holds it steady while I settle into the saddle, and he gives me a gentle push to send me on my way. In an instant I'm flying down the track that runs straight as a die between the potato fields, suddenly addicted to speed and the rippling of wind through my hair.

At the bottom where the track meets the road, I fall off. My right elbow is grazed and there's a cut on my left knee. Ignoring the pain, I try to get back on. I can't. Not without somebody holding the bike. I wheel it all the way back up the hill.

'What do you do at a T-junction?' I ask my husband.

Before I set off next time we have a discussion about the proper use of brakes and the right time to turn the handlebars.

At the bottom of the hill I fall off again. This time it's the other knee and a nasty bump on my shoulder. And I still can't get back on without help.

The third time I return black and blue my husband throws in the sponge and sells the bike.

He's only recently qualified as an engineer and I'm in my first year of teaching. Neither of us earns much money and often we're broke. Luckily the tenant farmer who's managing the land lets us help ourselves to leftover potatoes, and the barn's full of grain. We feed it to our ducks, and towards payday, live almost entirely on eggs and chips.

Our ducks are muscovies; black and white, hissers rather than quackers, smart and friendly. They're good layers too. At first their wings were clipped but now with feathers re-grown, they circle the house as soon as I let them out, and they perch in the trees. But even though they are able to fly, foxes have twice taken unwary dabblers in the daytime.

We have a string of brown-striped ducklings, so before leaving for work I set out water and grain in the old stone pigsty, where the little flock can safely await my return. At five o'clock I let them out to swim in the pond and search for worms in the long grass.

One chilly autumn afternoon the ducks waddle out of the pigpen as usual, but only two of the ducklings follow. The other four are lying in the water bowl, a huddled mess of bedraggled feathers. I quickly scoop them up, and using the bottom of my skirt, rub each little body dry. It's no use. They are ice-cold. Too young for their feathers to be oil-proofed, they've hopped into the bowl, become waterlogged, and have succumbed to hypothermia.

They're almost certainly dead, but I carry their limp bodies indoors. How can I warm them? Our only source of heat is the coal fire in the living room and that's not yet lit.

I run into the kitchen and turn on the electric stove. Then I lay the sad little bundles onto a baking tray, pop it into the oven and close the door. The glass window has discoloured with age so I can't see what's happening inside without releasing the heat. I wait, praying for a miracle. Five minutes pass.

There's a tiny squeak, and then another. I open the door and four perky little ducklings flutter onto the kitchen floor.

The prowler

We drive down to Yorkshire, and while my husband goes off to meet an old friend, I visit my mother at The Limes.

She puts on the kettle. 'How's school?' she asks.

I tell her about my new job – the headmaster's old-fashioned ways, the funny things my six-year-olds say. I stop short when I notice she's only half listening, and has a strained look on her face.

'Where's Grandma? I ask sharply. 'Is she sick?'

'No she's fine. She's upstairs having a rest, but she'll be down for supper.'

'So what's wrong?'

My mother hesitates. 'A man's been hanging around.'

'On the street?'

'No. In the garden. Twice last week I looked outside and thought I saw a movement, and then last night I spotted him standing under the apple tree.'

'What was he doing?'

'Staring up at me. When he realised I'd seen him he ducked down behind some bushes. Your grandmother was standing beside me and she saw him too, and now she's upset and keeps asking whether I think he'll try to break into the house.'

'Have you rung the police?'

'What's the point? Short of leaving an officer in the back garden all week, I doubt they'd have any chance of catching him.'

I don't know what to say. She might be right about the police. The man is probably just a prowler, a peeping Tom and not dangerous, but there's no way of knowing for sure. What sort of person creeps around in gardens at night frightening elderly women? I'm worried for them, and angry too.

At that moment my grandmother comes into the kitchen and we say no more. She sets the dinner plates on the table and my mother takes a shepherd's pie out of the oven. That's followed by apple crumble, and I offer to wash the dishes.

I've just taken a clean tea towel out of the drawer when I happen to glance outside. There, bathed in light from the window, a man is looking up at me.

Without a thought I burst out of the door and race down the steps into the darkness of the back garden. I see him – and run straight at him.

'Get out! Get out! How dare you!'

He turns, sprints for the fence and scrambles over the top. In an instant he's gone. I'm already walking back up the garden path when my mother comes running.

'You shouldn't have done that,' she cries. 'He might have had a knife. Anything could have happened.'

I know she's right. But she doesn't see her prowler again.

The butcher's son

The headmaster meets me at the gate with a tired smile, and offers to show me around the school. Judging by the lines on his face and the raised veins on the backs of his hands, he can't be far off retirement. Nor can the school by the look of it. There are cracks in the path, the building's stonework has blackened with age and paint hangs in ribbons from the rotting window frames.

We enter a dimly lit hall where sports equipment lies in a pile, and then go through a side door to cross a prison-like yard. At the far end there's a shabby portable containing two classrooms smelling of damp. The headmaster informs me that if I get the job one of them will be mine. Then he leads me back to his office to commence the formal part of the interview.

I explain how we've only recently moved to the Lake District where my husband has begun work on the new motorway. The headmaster in turn provides me with a history of this hundred-year-old school for boys in which, should I be offered the job, I would be the only female member of staff.

He gives me a brief description of the position and then asks about my teaching experience. Since leaving college I've only worked with six-year-olds. They were eager to learn and easy to control. I don't know how I'd go with a class of older boys. I confess as much to the headmaster. 'Maybe I'm not right for this,' I say. 'I'm not much of a disciplinarian.'

But he waves aside my misgivings, insists that I'm the ideal applicant and offers me the job. Buoyed by his confidence in me, and aware that the other available teaching position would involve an hour's travel over winding mountain roads, I decide to accept.

A few weeks later I'm surrounded by a pack of ruddy-cheeked country boys tearing around the classroom shouting obscenities at each other. When I demand they return to their places, they ignore me. Fortunately the headmaster has followed me into the room. He roars at them and they sit down.

'I'm warning you,' he says, pacing between the rows, 'if I hear from your new teacher that you've been misbehaving, there will be severe consequences. Severe.'

Then he shakes my hand, wishes me well and leaves. Immediately the boys twist around, slam down the lids of their desks and begin throwing mock punches at each other. I try to gain their attention but they scarcely acknowledge my presence, and their rowdy behaviour continues until the bell rings for break. By which time I'm a wreck.

The headmaster is on playground duty, leaving me to drink tea with the other member of staff, a round-faced man in his mid-forties.

'How are you doing in there?' he asks, studying my face with what seems like morbid curiosity.

I know he's heard the noise. Not wishing to appear incompetent on my first morning, I mumble something about how it will all be fine once I get to know the boys individually.

'I wouldn't bet on it,' he says. 'That lot know how to break a teacher. Their last one was a woman too. The only way she could make herself heard was by blowing her whistle in the classroom. She ended up leaving to have a nervous breakdown.'

My stomach lurches. 'What do you think I should do?'

'I don't know,' he says, 'but I have a whistle if you need one.'

Somehow I struggle through the remainder of the day. By home time I've received a string of abuse, doubt that anyone has learnt anything, and am acutely aware that unless I gain control quickly I may as well resign.

Shouting didn't help, so the next morning I begin by addressing the boys in a near-whisper. I tell them that in future, each interruption or use of bad language will result in five minutes detention at the end of the day. The boys look startled, stop what they're doing and settle down to their work. I realise I may have hit on something.

Peace reigns for half an hour, so towards the end of the lesson I decide to test my apparent success by inviting Lewis, the biggest, foulest-mouthed of the lot, to stand up and read out his essay to the class.

He gets up and tells me to fuck off.

'Right,' I say, as calmly as I can. 'You can sit down again now and stay behind five minutes after school.'

'Do you think I give a fuck about that?' he asks.

The class breaks into howls of laughter.

'Make that ten minutes,' I say.

The other boys look shocked, bow their heads and return to writing their essays. I pick up a piece of chalk and start putting sums on the blackboard, ready for the maths lesson.

When next I turn around, Lewis has moved to the back of the classroom and is in a conspiratorial huddle with three other boys who have also been thoroughly unpleasant. 'Return to your seat!'

He ignores me, so I award him another five minutes.

When the bell rings at the end of the day there's a rush for the door. I manage to waylay the four who've been given detentions and handing each a book to read, send them back to their desks. I check my watch carefully and in five minutes allow the first two to depart, and then in another five, one more. That leaves Lewis. Just then my co-teacher from next door enters the classroom.

He takes me aside. 'Why is he still here?' he whispers.

I tell him about my five-minute rule.

'How long have you given him?'

'It's added up to half an hour,' I say, sheepishly.

'Half an hour! You're brave. You obviously don't know Lewis's father. He's the local butcher. He's a real brute. I wouldn't want to be in your shoes tomorrow.'

With a sinking feeling I glance over at Lewis. I'm inclined to let him go, but if I do he'll know he's beaten me. I wait until the half hour is up before sending him home.

When I arrive the following morning he's waiting by the classroom door with a grim smile on his face. 'My dad's coming to see you today,' he says. 'And he's mad.'

With the class under threat of detention, the morning passes without incident and some of the boys even learn something. Then at eleven thirty the door opens and a man with the build of a Hereford bull bursts into the classroom.

'What the hell do you think you're doing, keeping my son back after school?' he roars, lunging at me with a pointed finger.

I step back, thoroughly alarmed. But when I hear the boys' delighted gasps, I've had enough. I look the man in the eye, reel off the list of four-letter words Lewis has called me, and demand to know what he intends to do about *that*?

The butcher's cheeks inflate like balloons and their colour changes from red to purple, and for an instant I fear for my life. Then he swings around and grabs Lewis by the ear.

'Wait till you get home,' he shouts, waving his fist in the boy's face. 'You're in for a thrashing.' Then he releases his son, gives me a quick nod, and makes for the door.

Since then Lewis has given me no further trouble and, surprisingly, he sees to it that no one else does either. I've become quite fond of my boys and I don't mind their rough country ways at all.

Running away

We live in a red-brick bungalow in the Eden Valley, on the northern fringe of the Lake District. It's an ordinary place, but the views are spectacular. As the sun drops behind the mountain in the evenings the paddocks turn to gold. Pheasants stalk the woodlands and there are salmon in the river.

At week's end we join my old college friends, Christine and Barry, to scramble up Gowbarrow Fell, or wander along the banks of Lake Ullswater where Wordsworth's daffodils grow. I pull on my hiking boots and although heavily pregnant, manage to climb over the mountains to Angle Tarn.

But now my husband's work on the motorway is nearing completion and when his father, an architect, asks him to join his company in Yorkshire, he agrees. It makes me sad to think that we'll soon leave the beauty of the Lake District to return to the West Riding's slag heaps and grime, although we won't be moving until after my baby is born.

My carefully laid plans for a home birth in the Lakes are thwarted when, weeks before time, I go into labour while visiting my mother in Yorkshire. With my pains coming at frequent intervals we hurry to the nearest maternity hospital.

I haven't booked a bed and the place is full. The nurse in charge makes it clear I'm not welcome, but grudgingly recognises it's too late to turn me away. A rapid birth is followed next morning by stitches – seventeen of them, sewn without anaesthetic by a doctor who shouts at me when I cry out in pain. I'm discharged with a beautiful baby boy we decide to call Angus.

Instead of returning to our home in the Lake District we go back to The Limes, where our son's cries wake my grandmother during the night. My husband, who has begun working with his father, scours the neighbourhood and finds a place that's available immediately. It's in a nearby town, on a small estate with A-shaped houses. He arranges for our furniture to be sent down from the Lake District, and when it arrives we move in.

Right away I'm unhappy there. A huge 'picture' window in the living room faces an identical one in the house opposite. The road between is so narrow that I can see the family eating dinner. And I know if I can look into our neighbours' living room they can look into mine. It makes me uncomfortable. I could draw the curtains but I don't want to sit in the dark.

We haven't been in the house long before I receive a complaint from the next-door neighbour. 'Either stop your dog barking or I'm going to the council,' he says, ambushing me when I'm at the gate.

'I'm sorry,' I say. 'It's hard to keep her quiet.' I fumble with the latch and try not to look into his flushed, angry face.

'Next time I hear her – that's it. I'll be on the phone.'

'I'm really sorry.'

'They'll have her put down, you know,' he retorts nastily, as I struggle to get the pram over the step and into the house.

He's right about the dog. Pebble barks if a car door slams. She barks if a stranger passes the house, and when the teenager who lives across the road starts up his motorbike.

When we lived in Armathwaite she roamed the paddocks, chased rabbits and dug holes. There was birdsong, the grunting of Edith, the neighbour's fat sow, the drone of a tractor ploughing a distant field. A lively young Dalmatian, she's cooped up all day in a small backyard where every noise is unfamiliar. Of course she barks. Yet somehow I must stop her, for I'm sure our neighbour means what he says.

And so a pattern unfolds. She goes outside to relieve herself. I hear her bark. I panic and drag her back inside. Then I wait for a knock at the door, the signal that a council official has come to take her away.

I wish I could return to our home in the hills, to the comforting care of the midwife who visited me during my pregnancy. I miss her wise advice. Mine is a tiny baby, born too soon. He cries piteously after every feed and no amount of gentle back-patting will release the bubble of wind in his tummy. Because of his colic he can only sleep for a few minutes at a time.

I become so exhausted I'm unsure whether I'm awake or asleep. When I do have the opportunity to rest I dream that I'm still nursing my baby. On waking I expect to find him in my arms and for one heart-stopping moment think I've dropped him.

And now the crying has begun. The tears run freely without reason. Ashamed, I hide myself away, and when Angus sleeps I sit motionless, staring at the wall.

My husband doesn't understand my misery. I can't blame him for that. I don't understand it either. I've nothing to do all day other than prepare his dinner and look after our beautiful baby boy who, despite his problems, is steadily gaining weight. Neither my relatives nor my husband's can explain my strange behaviour.

One evening when we're visiting his family, my father-in-law takes me aside. 'Pull yourself together,' he tells me.

I would, but I don't know how.

I struggle on until I can bear it no more. Then one evening, leaving my son with his father, I open the door and walk away.

My calves are scratched and bleeding, my feet are caked in mud and I've lost a shoe in a boggy ditch. It doesn't matter. I have escaped. For an hour I hurry on through the fields, neither knowing nor caring where I go.

Then at last I slow down, and my mind begins to clear. I know I never want to return to that A-shaped house. But as I stand among the stubble of that darkened field, one thought overrides all others – my baby son needs me. I have no choice. I must go back.

It occurs to me then that I'm lost. In the distance there's the yellow glow of a streetlight, so I set off towards it. As I draw nearer I see the field ends with a high stone wall, which I will have to climb to reach the road. I find a toehold, and after heaving myself up, swing my legs over the top and drop down to the pavement on the other side.

A man is standing directly in front of me.

I have just enough time to register fair hair and an army greatcoat before he reaches out and grabs me by the shoulder. Roughly drawing my body towards him, he presses his lips onto mine and kisses me fiercely. Shocked to the core and unable to conjure the strength to fight him off, I hang limply in his arms.

In a moment he releases his grip and steps back, staring at me intently. Then swearing under his breath, he crouches down and starts unlacing his heavy boots.

'Come here.' He clutches me around the waist and swings me onto the top of the wall. 'Give me your foot.' He makes a futile attempt to brush off the mud, then takes off his boots and pulls one and then the other over my ankles. When he's finished lacing them up, he asks, 'Which way's home?'

I slide down off the wall and point in what I think is the direction of my house. He takes my hand and I walk beside him like an obedient child.

Now and then I stumble because the boots are too big, but each time he catches me and won't let me fall. When we reach the railway bridge he stops. He takes a cigarette out of his pocket, strikes a match and cups his hands around the flame to protect it from the wind. By its light I can see the compassion in his face and I begin to feel a little easier.

'Did you know I was going to rape you?' he asks.

I nod dumbly.

'You looked so miserable that in the end I couldn't do it. Don't be frightened. I'll see you home safely.'

At the corner of the street I point out my house, and he stops.

'I won't come any farther. If your husband's at the door he might see me and guess what happened.'

Ignoring his protestations, I take off his boots and hand them to him. 'Thank you,' I say, tears in my eyes.

I wait until he's out of sight before I walk to our gate, then I go inside to where my baby son is waiting.

Sunset orange

After a brief survey of the house we go outside. A narrow path snakes between herbaceous borders and ends in a rose garden that covers at least a quarter of an acre.

'I promised the landlord you'd prune them. I told him you were a keen gardener,' says my mother-in-law.

I don't comment. We both know it's a lie. I haven't picked up a garden tool since I was small and did a bit of digging with my grandfather. But I'm grateful to her for finding this place, allowing us to escape from complaining neighbours and the A-line house's lack of privacy. I'll manage the roses somehow.

Three weeks later we move in. The rooms are of stately proportions with unfashionably high ceilings edged by a fancy cornice in a Grecian key pattern. Three steps and an ornate, wrought-iron balustrade divide the sunken lounge from the remainder of the living area. My grandmother would love the place, but it's dated and not to our taste at all. The rent's reasonable though, and our Dalmatian can run free. The adjoining garden is that of the landlord and he lives some distance away, between us and the main road.

One evening my husband says, 'To make the ceiling appear lower, we should paint it a darker colour than the rest of the room.' That sounds like good advice, and the following afternoon he arrives home carrying a pot of blue-black paint.

We borrow a couple of ladders and set about transforming the lounge. When we're done, the ceiling does seem lower and our starkly functional Scandinavian furniture no longer appears so out of place. Encouraged by our success, we walk into the bedroom where we stand before the bare white wall facing the window.

'It is a bit boring, isn't it,' I comment. Next day my husband brings home a pot of brilliant sunset-orange paint. It brightens the room tremendously.

For a month or so all is well, and we settle happily into our new home. But then one morning our neighbour (and landlord) catches me in the garden.

'It's high time you pruned the roses,' he tells me.

'Right,' I say. 'No problem.' I pick up the clothes basket and hurry back to the house.

When I see the landlord has gone, I walk down to the small steel shed beside the rose garden, open the door and peer inside. Behind the lawnmower, rakes, and a few pointed things I wouldn't know what to do with, I spy a pair of shears hanging from a hook.

I pick them up and soon I'm snipping away at the rose bushes, wishing I'd paid more attention when my grandfather pruned his. As I hack away, a few branches snap off but others only bend. The shears must need sharpening. I work for a while and then stop to consider whether I've cut off enough to satisfy the landlord. I study my work. Better call it a day.

A plum tree grows in the lawn near the washing line. My mother has given me a recipe for plum jam, so after I've hung out the nappies I check to see whether the fruit's ready for picking. There are wasps hovering around the tree and before I can move away one stings me on my top lip. The pain is bad enough but the swelling is worse, and within minutes my lip hangs down to my chin and I look like a tapir.

The wasps must have carefully timed their raid, for the following day I discover the plums have ripened to perfection. I ring my husband and ask him to buy some sugar on his way home from work so I can begin my jam making.

After I put down the phone I go into the kitchen intending to make a cup of tea. I'm filling the kettle when a movement outside the window attracts my attention.

It's the landlord. Pushing a wheelbarrow onto our front lawn.

Without further ado he sets about picking the plums, systematically removing all of the fruit and leaving none for me. I want to go outside and complain – after all, it's our tree isn't it? Then I remember my rose pruning issues and decide to leave well alone.

Although my husband says little, I can tell things are not going well for him at work. One evening he arrives home with the news that his father's firm is likely to go into liquidation and as a result he'll be out of a job. At once he dedicates himself to searching for a new position, but all the available engineering vacancies are in Birmingham, Manchester, and other heavily industrialised areas in which we have no desire to live.

Then one day he shows me an advertisement saying that the Qatar government is looking for engineers to build a sewerage system. But where is Qatar? We ring family and friends, but no one's heard of it. Finally, poring over an atlas, we discover the name written above a tiny pink dot on the edge of the Arabian Peninsula.

The conditions and tax-free salary sound excellent, so my husband attends an interview. When he's offered the position, we talk it over and decide to take this opportunity to explore a little-known part of the world and make money at the same time. As there's a probationary period he flies out first, leaving me to pack up and arrange for a removal van. A month later he phones to say all is well and Angus and I can join him in Qatar. I give notice to the landlord.

Shortly before it's time to leave, he knocks on the door and tells me he's come to inspect the house. Fortunately I've just tidied away my son's toys and the floor is freshly vacuumed. I invite him inside and follow him through the kitchen and then into the bedrooms.

He seems friendly enough, and it's not until he enters our room and sees the sunset-orange paint that his manner changes. To my surprise he doesn't like it at all. Maybe he's a bit old fashioned. He checks my son's bedroom, the bathroom and then the laundry.

When he steps into the living room his face turns the same colour as the bedroom wall. Whether it's the way he cranes his neck to look up at the blue-black ceiling I don't know, but he appears to be struggling for breath. He lets out a terrifying bellow and tells me that if I don't return it to its original white, he'll block the driveway and stop the removal van from leaving. Then he storms out, slamming the door behind him.

I'm shocked. The living room walls are immaculate because I washed them myself, and the ceiling looks lovely. I have a small child. I'm about to leave. It's too late to start painting.

But I know the landlord isn't an early riser, so I speak to the removalists who load the furniture and are gone before he's awake. And I know he won't find me in Arabia.

QATAR

The mud-brick house

It's a small, mud-brick house filled with the scent of Arabia: part dust, part sand, wood smoke, sewerage and spice. In the mornings I climb the internal stairway to the roof and listen to the *muezzin* calling from the nearby mosque. I watch the antics of the neighbour's goats and I can see the beds belonging to the migrant workers, placed where they'll catch the breeze.

I like our gate with its wrought-iron ornamentation and the privacy and security afforded by the high walls that surround the garden.

We don't have television but after dinner, as we sit and talk, we're entertained by the geckos chasing moths across the ceiling.

My husband, like everyone else, begins work in the early morning and finishes before the afternoon heat makes serious effort impossible.

When he's gone I make breakfast for myself and Angus, who is two and a half. First I measure out the milk powder and mix it with water. Next I pour it onto the cornflakes in our bowls and wait for the little black weevils to float to the surface. Then I scoop them off and we eat.

After breakfast Ali arrives and starts mopping the floors. He's a cheerful young man from Pakistan. I'm not accustomed to having servants, but with temperatures sometimes in the upper forties, I was told I'd need a houseboy to sweep and clean. A houseboy – I expected a teenager but got a man. Although he speaks few words of English, he smiles a lot and Angus likes him.

We did have a small misunderstanding early on, when I found a pile of paper and dust lying in the garden. 'Ali,' I asked, 'what do you do with the rubbish after you've swept the floor?'

By way of answer he smiled and showed me how he threw it out of the kitchen window.

Next day I told the story to a friend.

'That's nothing,' she said. 'It was months before I discovered my houseboy had been wiping the dishes with the same cloth he used for the lavatory.'

My next-door-neighbour, a journalist from Jordan, teaches me to make Turkish coffee. We cook together roasting eggplant on an open flame, rolling pine-nut-and-rice-filled vine leaves into tiny cigars. We make kibbeh, baba ghanoush and Lebanese dishes spiced with cardamom and tangy sumac. My favourite, fattoush, has pieces of toasted flatbread broken into mixed salad, dressed with sumac, garlic, olive oil and lemon.

The pedal car

While Ali washes the floors I go outside to water the garden. There's a narrow path around the house and beside it we've planted jasmine, cherry-pink oleanders and red-petalled hibiscus with long yellow stamens. We're growing citrus trees too, and as I spray them with water the air fills with the delicate scent of orange blossom.

Angus is round the back, pedalling his new red car. I can hear him making racing-car noises – zoom, zoom.

'Do you want me to bring you a drink?' I call out. 'I'm going inside to check on the potatoes. I don't want them to boil dry.'

It's safe to leave Angus alone in the garden because of its high walls, and I know he can't open the gate because I've tested him. I go into the kitchen and add more water to the pan. Then I pour orange juice into a glass and carry it outside.

'Angus! Where are you?'

Silence.

I walk around to the back of the house. He's not there. Feeling a twinge of anxiety, I run to the front and check the gate. It's firmly shut. Somehow our paths must have crossed and Angus has gone inside. He's playing in his bedroom.

No, he's not.

'Have you seen Angus?' I ask Ali.

He shakes his head.

Really frightened now, I rush to the gate, open it and run out into the road.

And there he is, some way off, earnestly pedalling his little red car towards me. He's accompanied by a bearded man wearing baggy trousers and the flat, pancake-like hat worn by the Pathans. I hurry down to meet them. I can see at once that Angus is enjoying his little excursion.

My son's new friend breaks into laughter. He points to the end of the street and by waving his arms around, shows me how Angus pedalled down the road and joined the other cars on the busy roundabout.

I'm shaken. I thank the man and offer him a drink, money – anything to show my gratitude, but he grins, shakes his head and walks away.

We're almost home when I notice a garbage cart standing beside the footpath. A man comes out of a nearby house carrying a bin on his shoulders. He empties it into his cart and then leans against it puffing on his cigarette, all the while leaving the neighbour's gate wide open.

Angus pedals his car back into our garden. I'm so relieved he's made it home safely that I can't even be angry with him.

Patterns in the rock

There are no fancy restaurants or indoor cinemas in Doha. Those Westerners who work for the oil company have their own pool and sporting facilities, but for the rest of us, our social life centres around a modest sailing club and whatever home entertainment we can devise.

We know all of the expatriates in Doha who drink and want to let off steam: the Lebanese, the Armenians and French, the Germans, Brits and South Americans, Singaporeans and Aussies. Between them they throw some wonderfully wild and varied parties – so good that no one wants to fly home for Christmas.

There's no work on Fridays, and in summer we sail or swim. Winter brings with it mild, balmy days, and we take our children into the desert to explore old forts or to slide down sand dunes on cheap tin trays.

We're heading north one afternoon, driving along a track parallel to the beach, when there's a flash of pink and we spot a dozen flamingos wading through the shallows. To our left a limestone outcrop rises from the sand, and we drive over and park beside it. The children in the group run off to play on its slopes while we adults lay out the rugs, unpack the picnic baskets and pour coffee.

Before we can drink it, Angus and his friend Hamish wave to us from the top of the hill and cry out, 'Come and see what we've found!'

I climb up the slope and the boys lead me to where a rectangle has been cut deep into the rock, perhaps for the purpose of catching rainwater. Strange indentations spread out around it – circles, and holes set out in rows, reminiscent of a board game the locals play. There are boat-shapes with what look like oars. I call out to my friends and for an hour we search the rocks, finding more and more carvings. Who would do this? And why?

As evening unfolds the wind stills, and the late-afternoon light casts a rosy glow onto the desert. I look out over its vast sameness and am reminded of how the Bedouin pick out subtle variations in the sand, recognising landmarks that we Westerners will never see.

It's time to pack up the picnic things and take our children home. The sun is going down and on our way back to the city we pass cars pulled over to the side of the road so their owners can turn to Mecca. They prostrate themselves on the ground and pray.

Later we ask our Qatari friends about the carvings in the rock but few have seen them. Those who have tell us they are very old, ancient even, but as to who made them or for what reason, they have no idea.

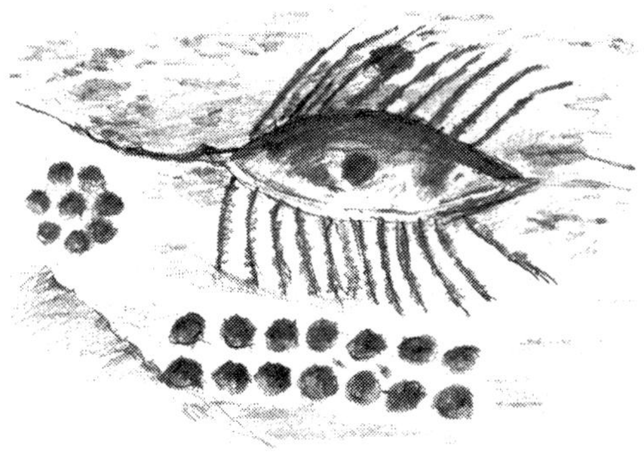

Oysters

'Do you like oysters?' my friend Vahé calls out to me from a blue-and-white speedboat lying off the beach.

'I think so,' I say.

'Come on then, we're ready to go,' says Daniel, who owns the boat.

I kick off my shoes and splash towards the two men through shallows so hot my feet tingle with the pain. Vahé reaches out his arms and heaves me over the side. Like a floundering haddock I flop into the bottom of the boat.

When I've more or less regained my dignity, Daniel starts the motor. He carefully manoeuvres around the swimmers and then heads out to sea. In a couple of minutes he turns the boat into the glass-calm channel that leads to the desalination plant, and cuts the engine. Then he strips off his shirt, dives in and vanishes into the blue-green depths.

I lean over the side, idly trailing my hand in water that glints like steel and wait for him to reappear. Time passes. I'm just beginning to worry when his shoulders break the surface. He tosses an oyster into the boat, takes a breath and plunges back into the sea.

When I was a child and on holiday with my mother in East Yorkshire, she bought two craggy, rock-like oysters from a seaside stall. Sold individually on little white saucers, they were expensive and considered a special treat. This oyster is different – flatter, soft-shelled and hairy.

Vahé picks up a knife with a curved blade and deftly levers it open. 'Try this,' he says, showing me the grey, translucent body.

I hesitate. I grew up eating tripe, pigs' feet, cows' heel and marrow bones on toast, but nowadays I'm squeamish. I'm disinclined to swallow this slimy, still-living animal plucked straight from the sea.

A minute later Daniel surfaces again and throws more oysters into the boat.

'How was it?' he gasps.

I have no choice. I slip the oyster out of its shell. When I bite down on it my mouth fills with creamy flesh bursting with flavor enhanced by the warm salt waters of the Arabian Gulf.

'It's fantastic.'

The two men laugh and clap their hands, then take turns diving for oysters until I can eat no more and have to beg them to stop.

A shared house

I'm in the bathroom rinsing sand out of our bathers after an afternoon at the sailing club, when the phone rings.

It's my mother. 'Your grandmother's had a stroke,' she says. 'I don't think she's going to make it.'

I tell my husband and he goes straight to the phone to arrange seats for me and Angus, now three, on the next plane back to England. It's upsetting to hear that my grandmother is dying, but the news isn't entirely unexpected. She's been unwell for some time. And she's ninety-four. I throw a few clothes into a bag and soon after we're in the air, heading to Heathrow.

Grandma's still living when we arrive, but she sleeps all the time and my mother tells me she hasn't spoken in days. We tiptoe into her room. As Angus approaches her bed she wakes up, laughs and reaches out to him, and I'm glad we made it home in time. From then on my mother and I take it in turn to watch over her, but she doesn't open her eyes again and in a few days she's gone.

Shortly after, amid the pain of her loss, Angus and I fly back to Qatar, leaving my mother alone at The Limes.

In accordance with my grandfather's will, the house now passes to my aunt, but she won't be able to sell it until after probate. It will be several months before my mother has to move out but I've no idea where she'll go then.

A few weeks after our return to the Gulf, I call her. She must be getting anxious. I know I am.

The phone rings for a while before my mother picks it up.

'Sorry,' she says, 'I was upstairs sorting out bed linen, ready for when I move.'

'Move where?' I ask, surprised.

She tells me how her friend Jean has seen a place she would like, but can't afford. 'She's suggested we buy it between us.'

'But how would you pay the deposit? And your half of the mortgage?'

'We won't need one. We'll buy it outright. She'll have the money from her old place, and I've spoken to your father. He's promised to pay my share. He said I should go right ahead. Wait till you see the house – you'll love it!'

I sigh. 'Just a minute, Mum. This isn't going to happen.'

'Of course it is. Your father's sending the agent my half of the deposit this week. It'll be here on Thursday.'

I'm shocked. Have I been wrong about him all these years?

'There's room for you all to stay when you come home on leave. It's in a nice quiet street within walking distance of the bowling club. The garden's beautiful. There's an apple tree in the corner and a trellis against the fence, covered in little pink roses.'

'How wonderful,' I say, thinking this sounds almost too good to be true.

The next time I call, she tells me, 'I've decided to sell the half-poster bed, the oak table in the front room and Grandpa's roll-top desk, and I'm going to use the money to buy a new armchair and a nice coffee table.'

My mother and her friend have agreed on how to arrange the furnishings, and by the sound of it they'll live harmoniously together.

Then late one evening my mother calls to tell me she's moved in.

'I'm so pleased for you,' I say. 'To be honest, when you told me about the house I didn't think this would happen. I couldn't imagine my father coming up with the money.'

'Actually he hasn't yet, but it's nothing to worry about. There's been a small hitch, but he's expecting to have it all sorted out within the next few days.'

I wince. 'Hang on. You said you've moved in. How could you do that if my father hasn't paid?'

'It wasn't a problem. I told Jean about the little delay and she used her savings to cover my share. I'll pay her back in a week or so.'

I'm horrified.

There's a moment's silence, and then my mother says brightly, 'I'm going to love living here and there's absolutely nothing for you to worry about.'

But I *do* worry and, as it turns out, with good reason. After a few months, when my father's money still hasn't arrived, the house has to be sold and the two women never speak to each other again.

Fortunately, just as my mother is about to become homeless, an old family friend who usually lives in Italy returns home for a visit. She owns several properties and immediately offers one at a peppercorn rent. It's an old 'two up and two down' at the far end of our street. My mother, who by now is desperate, accepts gratefully and my 'aunt' arranges for an indoor bathroom to be installed upstairs.

So my mother packs her share of the furniture and moves into the little miner's cottage. I visit her the next time we're home on leave, and I've never seen her happier.

Cockroaches

The morning after we move from our mud-brick home to a new, modern house with tiled floors, I discover an animal in the kitchen. A glossy brown beetle is sitting on the draining board, sunning itself under the window. I'm surprised. Since coming to Qatar I've seen little insect life, and assumed the climate was too hot and dry for anything but scorpions and the odd fly.

The creature, which must be at least an inch-and-a-half long, acknowledges my presence with a gentle wave of its feelers. I haven't seen anything like it before, but whatever it is, it can't stay in the house. I carefully wrap the beetle in a cloth, carry it outside and release it under the red-flowering hibiscus by the front gate. And then I forget about it.

A week later there's a power cut in the middle of the night. That's a common happening on hot summer evenings when the power station can't cope with the load. We're woken by the thump of the air conditioner coming to an abrupt halt and within minutes the temperature in the house shoots up. My skin prickles with perspiration and I throw off the sheets. Unable to sleep, I toss and turn for an hour until, miraculously, the power comes back on. Feeling thirsty, I get up and walk through to the kitchen, enjoying the cool feel of the terrazzo tiles under my feet.

At the door I sense movement. I pause. When I click on the light there's pandemonium. Hordes of brown beetles scatter in every direction over benchtops, cooker and cupboards, bashing into each other in their panic. For a moment there's chaos – then they're gone. I fill a glass with water and go back to bed, shaken.

Next day I ask an 'Old Gulf Hand' about these alarming night-time visitors.

'They're cockroaches,' he tells me. 'I can't believe you've lived here a year and not come across them. Just use fly spray and make sure you squirt some down the drains. Oh, and don't forget to put the plug into your sink before you go to bed.'

We follow his sound advice.

The following morning I'm sitting naked on the toilet enjoying a few moments of quiet reverie when I'm dive-bombed.

Nobody told me cockroaches could fly. The beastly thing flutters around my head, bashing itself against the walls of the tiny room and sending me into total panic. I jump up and lash out at it with my sandal. There's a loud plop, and grey roach innards burst onto my face and neck. Shrieking, I rush into the bathroom and turn on the shower. It's a while before I feel clean again.

It doesn't matter that they don't sting or bite; from now on cockroaches are the enemy. I lie in ambush in the kitchen, flashing on the light at varying times during the evening, vigorously squirting anything that moves. The creatures have a primeval resilience and refuse to die. Hours after I've sprayed them I find their serrated legs frantically clawing the air. I feel sorry for their suffering, but at the same time I'm revolted.

We take to shaking out our shoes before putting them on, and checking between the sheets before we get into bed. I'm aware that I'm becoming paranoid. I can't even have a quiet after-dinner drink with my husband without surreptitiously scanning the dark corners of the room.

Sometimes I forget. I reach into the wardrobe one evening, take out a paisley print dress I haven't worn for a while and slip it over my head. It's a bit tight. I tug at the hem and slide my fingers over the silky material, smoothing out the creases.

It's then that I feel the gentle caress of hairy feet against my skin. I shudder and the cockroach loses its grip. It falls to the floor and scuttles into my son's bedroom.

When I tell my friends about our infestation I discover an emerging folklore. Everyone wants to tell me about their own cockroach experience, each more horrific than the last. One ghoulish friend describes how the creatures climb into cots during the night to suck the exudations from the eyes of sleeping children.

I have to destroy that beast in my son's room. My problem is that in there I'd rather not use the only spray we have available, because I've seen the huge list of chemicals it contains. What is dichlorodiphenyltrichloroethane?

The streets of Doha are deserted in the sweltering heat of the day, and it's not until a cool breeze arises at sundown that Qatari families emerge from the refuge of their homes. They walk along the Corniche, take their children to the park or browse through the stalls in the *souq*. So on a pleasant evening when I'm driving to the Shell Club for a game of badminton with friends, everyone is out on the street.

By the time I reach the town's main roundabout where a fountain plays under gaudy fluorescent lights, the traffic is heavy. I succeed in squeezing between a truck and a rusty old utility with two fat-tailed sheep in the back, but before I can take the turnoff for the club, something causes me to look downward.

My heart jolts. An enormous black cockroach is walking up my right leg, heading purposefully towards the hem of my little pleated tennis skirt. Desperately trying to shake off the disgusting thing, I lose control of the car and it swings sideways. The old Bedouin in the ute screams and blasts on his horn, bringing me to my senses. Narrowly avoiding a collision, I pull over.

In the morning my husband speaks to the Sanitary Department, and later in the day our bell rings and I find three young men waiting at the gate. Their English is limited, but they are all smiles and reassurance. Waving their hands around, they explain that they have come to fix our cockroach problem.

I look at them doubtfully. I would have expected overalls, but instead they are neatly dressed in white shirts, dark trousers and thongs.

'Where's your equipment?' I ask.

'No, no need.' The man thrusts a small package towards me. 'Bomb,' he says.

They walk around to the back of the house where there's a pit covered by a heavy metal grate. They prize it open.

'Go inside,' one says, shooing me towards the back door.

I go into the kitchen, where I lean over the sink to watch events through the window. The man with the bomb drops it into the pit. Then all three remove their thongs and gripping one in each hand, crouch at the edge of the hole.

Nothing happens.

After a minute or so, the bomber bends down and peers into the darkness. He leaps back as a brown river of cockroaches flows over the edge of the pit and spreads out across the concrete. The three spring into action, using their thongs to flatten every beetle within reach. Then they put on their shoes and chase after those that have escaped – stamping, laughing and shouting out to each other. It's a party, a wild, crazy dance.

When they are done, hundreds of cockroaches lie dead in the sunshine. The men from the Sanitary Department leap up and down, hugging each other like footballers who've won the finals. Then they bang on the back door, eager to have me see what they've achieved. I dutifully admire the bodies and then pour out three iced glasses of orange juice.

We rarely see a cockroach now – but I dream of them.

Desert picnic

Our Qatari friends may work in offices but they are Bedouin at heart and take every opportunity to go out to the desert. One Friday they invite us to join them and to bring along a young engineer who recently arrived from England.

When we reach the site of our 'picnic' we see a tent has been erected. Huge cauldrons are heating over charcoal fires, and in one a whole sheep is being boiled.

After a few minutes the cooks pile a mountain of rice onto a metal platter. They heave the sheep onto it, and top the dish with the yellow fat of the tail. Then they lay it on the ground in front of the tent and our host invites us to sit in a circle around it.

We have told our new friend about Qatari etiquette, warning him it's bad manners to expose the dirty soles of one's feet to fellow diners. For women that's easily avoided. I can sit however I choose and hide my feet under the folds of my caftan. It's not so simple for European men who are wearing trousers and are unaccustomed to sitting cross-legged.

No cutlery is provided, just the knife that our host uses to slice off the best parts of the sheep for us, his honoured guests. Having been on several desert picnics before, I know to use my right hand for eating since the left is officially reserved for ablutions. I squeeze the rice into a ball with my fingers and pop it into my mouth. It's been cooked with whole dried limes and fragrant spices, and is delicious. After a while I glance across to where the new engineer is sitting. He's shifting about uncomfortably in a ring of rice that has failed to reach its destination.

When we've finished eating we are offered coffee. Cardamom pods are added to the brew, making *gahwa* an acquired taste, but its serving to guests is integral to Qatari hospitality and it should not be refused.

I look across at the new engineer who has just been presented with his first cup of *gahwa,* and I can tell that although he's trying to be polite, he's having a hard time swallowing it. But he polishes it off somehow, and when our host offers him another, he shakes his head and hands the man his empty cup. It's refilled immediately and given back to him.

No! We didn't warn him about that.

Looking decidedly unhappy, our friend gulps down his second cup of *gahwa.* The next time our host returns with his brass coffee pot he tells him firmly that he definitely doesn't want any more, and hands back the cup. It's filled again and pressed into his hands, and I see the first signs of panic. We take pity on him and explain how, by gently shaking his cup, he can indicate to his host that he's had enough. Probably for a lifetime.

Back in the USSR

It's high summer and after twelve months in Qatar, time to escape the heat and go on leave. We'd like to make the most of our free tickets by having a stopover on the way back to the UK. But where should we go?

We think of Italy, or Yugoslavia, but as we pore over the map we notice that it's dominated by a large pink area to the north – the Soviet Union. There have been frightening stories about life behind the Iron Curtain, but are they true or only Western propaganda?

After thinking it over we decide to find out for ourselves, and apply for visas. We are told then that we must pay for the entire holiday in advance. Intourist, the state-run travel agency, sends us a book of coupons to be used in lieu of money.

Our Armenian friends talk longingly of the homeland they will never be able to visit, and it makes us think we'd like to begin our holiday there. First though, we must fly to Lebanon, from where we can pick up a flight to Yerevan, the Armenian capital.

The seats on the plane out of Beirut are mainly filled with elderly couples, men in waistcoats and women wearing headscarves and long black dresses. We're the only Westerners on the flight. It's only two hours to Yerevan, and soon we're in the terminal building nervously awaiting the scrutiny of the Soviet immigration officials.

It's a pleasant surprise when our passports are accepted and stamped without incident. Then we're ushered into a small customs hall where we join the other passengers crowded together on wooden benches, awaiting the arrival of their luggage. Within minutes the first suitcase is brought in. An immaculately uniformed officer picks it up, turns it upside down and dumps the entire contents onto a table. Every article is opened, taken apart, sniffed, and meticulously examined. Time passes.

When a second, and then a third bag receive the same lengthy treatment, our hearts sink. It could be hours before everyone's luggage is processed. It's been a long day. Angus is tired, bored and restless. I give him the model plane we bought in Beirut and pray that our suitcases will be next.

With no access to food or water, and after three hours in a hot room, one of the old ladies passes out. Her son picks her up, props her back on the bench and tries to keep her cool by fanning her with a newspaper. Another hour goes by. Then miraculously our bags appear. To our surprise they receive only a cursory glance and in no time at all we're outside, gulping in the fresh air.

We've been told by Intourist that transport to the city will be provided and sure enough, an official directs us to a coach waiting in front of the main building. It's empty and there's no sign of the driver, but a helpful policeman gestures that we should get on anyway.

Twenty minutes go by, and then two Armenians climb the steps, walk to the back of the bus and sit down. There's another twenty-minute wait before the arrival of a second couple. It's then that we realise the awful truth – we'll have to wait for a whole busload of passengers to go through customs before the coach leaves for Yerevan.

Eight hours after our arrival we reach the city and are dropped off in front of our hotel. At reception we're asked for our passports – which are instantly confiscated. Not yet seasoned travellers, we are nevertheless aware of the cardinal rule that you should never let your passport out of your sight.

Our objections are coldly ignored.

The room is adequate. Not that we care. It has beds, and that's enough. In the morning I open the net curtains and look down onto a tree-lined square where elderly women sweep the pavements with old-fashioned brooms. We dress and go downstairs to the breakfast room, smiling politely at our fellow guests. They don't respond and we eat our toast marooned in a sea of stony expressions.

As we eat we discuss the situation and quickly come to the conclusion that we're embarking on the holiday from hell. We don't care about the pre-paid coupons. We'll cut short our trip and catch the next flight out. After breakfast we go to reception, tell the Intourist guide we're leaving, and ask for our passports.

'You have arranged to stay in the Soviet Union for two weeks and you must stay for two weeks,' she tells us icily. 'Your passports will not be returned until you have completed your holiday.'

She makes it sound like a prison sentence.

Shocked by this news, and concerned about the lack of fresh milk for Angus, we walk outside and go in search of a grocer's. As far as we can tell we're not being monitored and can roam around the town without restriction. We enter a shop where partially filled shelves sport a few rows of canned goods and the odd pair of socks, but no fresh milk. Then in a corner I spy three tins of condensed milk, so we join the queue leading to the counter.

After a long wait it's our turn. I point to the cans and take out my purse. Instead of handing me the milk the shop assistant scribbles on a strip of paper, gives it to me, and indicates we must now join the back of another equally long queue leading up to a cash register.

Half an hour later we succeed in paying for the milk. We return to the end of the original queue, which by now has grown even longer. Eventually we reach the front, I show the receipt to the first assistant and she gives me the cans. The morning has gone.

A few days later we're on a plane again, this time on our way to Tbilisi, the capital of Georgia. It's our first experience of flying within the Soviet Union. A formidable stewardess with great meaty arms serves us a glass containing something pale and fizzy, which tastes suspiciously like Epsom salts. Although I'm thirsty I hesitate to drink it. I've already been to the lavatory and I know there's no toilet roll.

Tbilisi is beautiful. It's perched on the banks of a river and is surrounded by snow-capped mountains. Our guide, who speaks perfect English, shows us around the city and takes us to see ancient, gold-encrusted

icons. On the way he tells us he is studying medicine. He's unhappy that once qualified he could be sent to live anywhere in the Soviet Union, and quite possibly to Siberia.

A few days later we're in Moscow, standing in the vastness of Red Square in a pale dawn. As we watch, shafts of sunlight break through the mist and illuminate the glittering domes of St Basil's Cathedral. Although it's early, there's already a line of people filing past Lenin's tomb. The queue stretches across the square and into a nearby park where it fills all the little laneways. The people shuffle forward one slow step at a time, waiting to honour the founder of their revolution, even if it takes all day.

We are booked into the Hotel Berlin, possibly the most lavishly decorated hotel in all of Russia. Painted cherubs chase each other across the dining-room ceiling and we sit among its gold-encrusted pillars, listening to the trickling of a fountain.

The waiter hands us an enormous menu and goes away. Relieved to see it's printed in English as well as Russian, we scroll through pages of caviar, stuffed quails, marrons glacé and other exotic delicacies. After some time spent mentally tasting this gastronomic compendium, we look around for someone to serve us. The waiter is now standing in front of a side table, polishing glasses. I beckon politely. He doesn't respond. I call out. He takes no notice. Then he disappears, leaving us in splendid isolation.

When we're convinced that we are to be left forever to our own devices, the room suddenly fills with noise. A party of jovial East Germans appears and fills both sides of a long table to our right. Two waiters emerge from the kitchen carrying steaming bowls of soup, with which they quickly serve the twenty or so waiting diners. We look on, dumbfounded.

After the last bowl is delivered, and before the waiters can escape, we succeed in waylaying one and demand to be fed. Scowling, he points at the menu and asks us what we want. My husband picks out half a dozen offerings in turn, but at every suggestion the man shakes his head and repeats brusquely, 'Not available.'

Running out of steam and half starved, I finally ask, 'What is on the menu?'

'Beef soup.'

'Right,' I say. 'We'll have that.'

The following morning we search for souvenirs in Gum, a massive department store facing Red Square. Our time in the Soviet Union is coming to the end, and a couple of days later we check out of the hotel and are ushered onto the airport coach. At immigration our passports miraculously reappear and are duly stamped. For the first time we see other tourists from the West, waiting in the terminal.

But where is the plane? Departure time comes and goes. Hours pass. We try to find out why our flight is delayed, but no one seems to know. Then just as we're losing hope of ever getting out of Moscow, its number is called. The gates open and we're ushered onto a crowded bus.

It takes us across the tarmac and stops beside the plane. The driver gets out and we wait for the door to open. We wait. And we wait. It's summer. It's hot inside the bus. We're crushed together and we're sweating. We have a little boy with us. After a while our driver reappears, gets back on the bus and without explanation returns us to the terminal.

By evening we're desperate. When we see that some passengers have succeeded in waylaying an official, we hurry over.

'Your plane won't be leaving tonight,' he tells everyone. 'Tomorrow perhaps?'

I'm outraged by the lack of information, but the Russians among us appear unsurprised and are apparently accustomed to long delays and indifference. Now we'll have to return to Moscow and spend another night in our hotel.

Wrong. At the door of the terminal we're stopped by a policeman.

'Your passports have been stamped,' he says. 'You are no longer in the Soviet Union. If you wish to return you will need to apply for a visa.'

Having spent hours trying to stop a small child from cracking up, I'm now close to a breakdown myself. Suddenly my voice can be heard all over the airport, shrilly insisting, 'Someone *do* something!'

Passengers put down their luggage and turn around, looking shocked. It seems no one ever makes a fuss or draws attention to herself in the Soviet Union. Amazingly though, it works. A Red Army officer rushes us out of the terminal and in no time at all we're back at the hotel.

In the morning our trusty Intourist guide returns us to the airport. There are no further delays and in a relatively short time we're on a flight to London, being served caviar and champagne by a svelte Aeroflot stewardess.

I sit with Angus, and my husband is across the aisle. When we look over at each other we discover to our surprise that we could now be mistaken for Russians. Our faces bear the same stony expressions that have surrounded us for the last two weeks.

The coup

I'm making our bed when the phone rings. It's my friend, Jenny.

'There's been a coup,' she announces.

'A what?'

'A coup. You know, where there's some sort of civil war thing and a new ruler takes over. Ian's phoned from work to tell me.'

Right away I start to giggle. I can't help myself. The thought of it is ridiculous. Qatar's a pleasant, quiet country with next to no crime. We've lived here for two years and Doha's our home town; a familiar, comfortable place in which to raise our son. The notion of a coup happening in Qatar is as outrageous as suggesting there's one occurring in Blackpool.

'It's no laughing matter,' says Jenny severely. 'I've had a call from the kindergarten. That's why I'm ringing you. We're to pick up the kids right away. And after that make sure you stay inside and lock the doors.'

I don't think this is anything to get excited about, so I spend a little time brushing my hair and putting on lipstick before I go out to the car. I haven't had it long. An Opel GT in silver-grey with crimson-leather seats, it's far more dashing than anything I've owned before – the sort of car sheiks' sons like to drive.

I'm nearly in town when I remember reading about coups in other faraway places; of roving gangs armed with machetes and terrified expatriates hiding under their beds. But they were in the riskier parts of Africa, to which we wouldn't go for a visit, let alone to work and live.

In Doha there are the usual townsfolk on the streets, their arms

filled with flat bread and great bunches of mint and parsley to make into tabbouli. A queue has formed outside the butcher's and, as always, a million flies are buzzing around a bloody carcass hanging by the door. Three men are standing outside the barber's waiting to be shaved. Perhaps it's a false alarm.

I drive on past the timber and cardboard shacks of migrant workers who live on the edge of town, and then leaving the traffic behind, travel along the newly built outer ring road. To my left the desert stretches to the horizon with only an occasional thorn bush to break its monotony, and I blink in the sharp light reflected off the sand.

I'm approaching the turnoff for the kindergarten when there's a deafening roar and the car shakes. Alarmed, I turn my head and see a man, a European, looking out at me from the cockpit of a jet fighter. In a flash he's gone. Shaken, I swing off to the right at the next roundabout and two minutes later park in front of the school.

'I've just been buzzed by one of those Harrier jump jets,' I tell my son's teacher.

She stares at me. I don't stop to explain and hurry Angus out to the car. Aware now of the risks involved in being mistaken for a fleeing member of the royal entourage, I avoid the ring road and go home a different way. And we forego our usual afternoon swim at the sailing club.

That evening we turn on the radio and listen to the Qatar National News. Sheik Ahmed has been deposed by his cousin, Sheik Khalifa bin Hamad al Thani. Apparently there's been an announcement informing members of the public service and military that they will receive an immediate and substantial pay rise if they swear allegiance to the new sheik.

In the morning the coup, which has been timed to coincide with one of Sheik Ahmad's overseas trips, is over, and without a drop of blood being shed.

A few days later we receive panicked calls from relatives in England who have just found out about it. By then our life has already returned to its normal pattern of work, afternoon nap, swim or sail at the club, dinner, and perhaps a little shopping in the cool of the evening.

Mr Muckerjee's shop

We buy our dry goods from Mr Muckerjee. It's always a pleasure to visit his shop. He greets us at the door with a warm smile, and with a gracious sweep of his arm, ushers us inside. Angus loves going to the shop, for into his small hands Mr Muckerjee slips Turkish delight flavoured with rosewater and pieces of halva dripping in honey.

While he keeps our son entertained, we squeeze between the vats of pink-pickled turnip and olives flavoured with lemon, and search for powdered milk or canned goods from Egypt and Lebanon. At the rear of the shop a second door leads into a dimly lit room smelling of cumin and cardamom, where bags of rice, chickpeas and dried limes are stacked to the ceiling.

After we've found what we want, we stand beside the counter gossiping with Mr Muckerjee while he packs our groceries into paper bags. He sends his boy outside to load them into our car. If then a wallet should be pulled out, he at once waves it away.

'No. No need to pay today,' he tells my husband. For Mr Muckerjee believes an Englishman's word is his bond, and allows the hundred or so Westerners who live in Doha to run up enormous bills without once reminding them of their debt.

We're eating breakfast one morning when I notice the powdered-milk tin is empty. I tell Angus to put on his shoes and we drive around to Mr Muckerjee's. For once he isn't at the door to greet us but we go inside and I soon find a tin of Nido. Then, while Angus plays with a little Chinese puzzle lying on the counter, I check the shelves for anything new or interesting that might have recently arrived in Doha. When, after a few minutes Mr Muckerjee still hasn't appeared, I wander through to the room at the back. It's spanned by a broad wooden beam.

Mr Muckerjee is hanging from the beam.

I take one look, grab Angus and rush for the door. Then I stop to take a breath, wondering what on earth to do. Before I can decide, someone behind me touches my arm, and a voice asks, 'Is anything wrong?'

It's Mr Muckerjee!

'For a moment I thought you were dead,' I say, staring at him.

He appears taken aback, puzzled by my obvious distress. Then a knowing smile breaks across his face. 'Ah, you saw my rope contraption, isn't it? I've a bad back you know. I find hanging to be very relieving.'

Nervous travellers

We're taking a short break and flying across the Gulf to Iran with another couple whose children are about the same age as Angus. I'm looking forward to the trip but I'm nervous.

It's a fortnight since members of the Popular Front for the Liberation of Palestine hijacked five jets, landed them on Dawson's Field in Jordan and then blew them up. One plane, a BOAC VC10 was returning to London from Bahrain, which is a short flight from where we live in Doha. Being regular travellers ourselves, we felt keenly for the passengers stranded for days in the searing heat of the desert, unaware they would eventually be released.

When we arrive at the airport in Doha I realise we're not the only ones spooked by recent events, for both our documents and our suitcases are checked and re-checked.

This will be our first visit to Iran, and it's a country we know little about. Ahead of us in the queue stand a dozen young men, itinerant workers returning home. They are all dressed alike in white shirts and black trousers. Each man carries a bag and two umbrellas. Why two? Does it rain a lot in Iran? They seem odd souvenirs to take home from Qatar, one of the driest countries on earth.

I'm the first of our party to climb the steps to the rear of the plane. Before I can take my seat I'm stopped in the aisle by an air hostess who insists on a final security check. It's a 'pat down'. The Iranian workers swing their heads around to watch the Western woman being felt all over – and I am utterly humiliated.

After a short flight we arrive in Shiraz. We go through customs, find a taxi, and drive along wide, tree-lined boulevards to our hotel. I'm struck by the sight of roses growing in profusion. An hour ago we were in the desert.

Our driver tells us Shiraz is known for its roses and nightingales, its wine and most particularly for its poets. In Europe, streets and squares commonly bear the names of military figures or famous battles. In Shiraz, where the inhabitants value poetry, hotels, boulevards and even tea houses are named for Ferdowsi, Sa'di and Omar Khayyam.

We wander through the bazaar admiring the carpets, and then take a taxi to the Shah Cheragh shrine. We've been told it's important to Shia Muslims, and when we arrive hundreds of pilgrims are gathered outside. As non-Muslims we don't expect to be allowed in. But two elderly ladies come up to me and my friend Jenny, and loan us lengths of cloth with which to cover our heads and bodies. Then they welcome us inside to view the shrine's glittering walls, entirely covered in mirrored mosaic. We learn that Shah Cheragh means 'King of the Light'.

Hafez, a renowned fourteenth-century poet, is buried in Shiraz and we visit his tomb. It's in the centre of a garden, and Iranian visitors recite his verses while wandering down pathways edged with flowers. We walk beside tranquil pools and flowing streams in the shade of carefully tended orange trees.

Next morning we drive to Persepolis. If this ancient city was in Italy or

Greece it would be thronging with tourists, but there are no Westerners here and only a few Iranians. We gaze in awe at the monumental doorways, gigantic columns and well-preserved stone reliefs.

A day later we travel over the mountains to Isfahan, passing through villages clinging onto rocky outcrops. Children and rough-coated sheep dogs rush out to greet us.

Isfahan is a stunningly beautiful city. Mosques, bazaars and caravanserais surround a massive square where once the Shah watched polo being played. Thousands of blue tiles decorate the roofs and domes and sparkle in the sunshine.

In the bazaar we're half-deafened by the sound of hammers beating out dainty patterns on copper and pewter. Craftsmen show us how the finest carpets are designed, woven and cut, and we watch old men painting miniature hunting scenes onto mother of pearl.

Our taxi driver offers to take us to see the minarets of the Manar Jomban tomb. When we arrive we're not especially impressed. They seem ordinary compared with those we've already seen in Isfahan and Shiraz, but we follow our guide up to the flat roof of the mausoleum.

He persuades us to climb the claustrophobically narrow stairway to the top of one of the minarets.

I'm admiring the view and feeling only slightly insecure, when the man repeatedly throws himself against the wall, causing the tower to sway alarmingly.

'Look! Look!' he says, pointing across the roof to the other minaret.

That one is rocking too. Thoroughly shaken myself, I dash down the steps to safety.

Much later I learn that the minarets were designed by a famous mathematician and Iranians have been shaking them for the last 200 years.

With suitcases and bags weighed down with copper lamps, rugs and craftwork, we prepare to fly home. For days we've been surrounded by gardens, greenery and breathtaking scenery, and I'm loathe to return to the desert. At the last moment I stop to buy my own special memento – an oval tin filled with delicate pink and white cyclamen.

As we arrive at the airport our concerns about hijacking re-emerge and I look nervously at the other passengers lining up at customs. A security official picks up a knife and pokes my tin of cyclamen, checking for a bomb or grenade, but when he doesn't find one I'm allowed to take it onto the plane.

We've been home for a day when the flowers drop off. I investigate the soil inside the tin and discover that each corm has been chopped into a dozen pieces. I throw them away.

Dhows

In the evenings we park beside the Doha Corniche and walk towards the harbour, where we watch the fishermen repairing their nets. There's often a *dhow* under construction, its teak frame expertly sculpted by workers who use only hand tools: an adze, saw and bow drill. They build strong, beautifully proportioned boats without ever referring to a plan, and their skill is handed down from generation to generation.

Our friends hire a *dhow* one afternoon and we're thrilled when they invite us to join them on board. The captain shows us around. He talks of pearl diving in earlier times, and of carrying cargoes of fresh water, fruit and frankincense throughout the Arabian Gulf and down the African coast.

Then he says, 'If anyone needs to use the lavatory . . .' and points to the thunder box, a wooden construction with a hole in its centre that hangs off the side of the boat. I take one look and resolve not to drink too much. One of the crew starts up the diesel engine and soon we're speeding through the water leaving the dusty town behind.

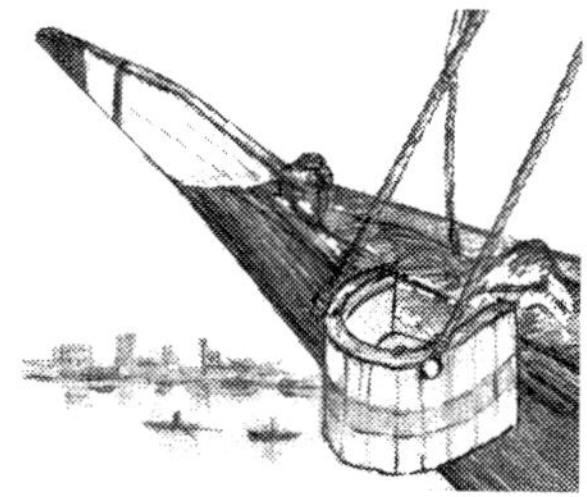

When we're well out to sea, we ask if the sail can be raised. It seems it's rarely used now, the engine having made it redundant, but the captain understands our desire to experience the romance of the old days, and soon the huge triangular canvas is billowing above our heads. At once we enter a quieter, calmer world where there are only the seagulls' cries, the sound of the waves splashing against the boat's sides, and the creaking of the deck beneath our feet.

In an hour the crewmen turn the *dhow* into the wind and hand out baited lines. I'm new to fishing but I haven't had my line in the water for more than two minutes when I feel something bite. Excited, I succeed in landing my first fish, a small shark. Within seconds everyone is frantically heaving on their lines too. We pull a dozen sharks on board and the men slash at them with curved knives. The deck is awash with their blood, but still the fish thrash around in their agony and refuse to die.

Then the sail is lowered and we motor back to the harbour where I thank the captain and our friends. I won't forget the pure joy of skimming through blue waters on a *dhow* in full sail.

But I'll never go fishing again.

Death in the desert

A week later I'm sitting on the beach at the sailing club, watching Angus run in and out of the shallows while I chat with my friend. Her son, who is a year younger than mine, is playing in the sand in front of us, filling a bucket and turning out sandcastles.

A man approaches. She smiles and it seems she knows him well. He crouches down to speak to her. He tells her that an hour ago her husband rolled his car on the North Road. And he's dead.

On the day of the funeral we follow a slow trail of cars out of town to where a plot of land has been set aside for Christian burial. Camel thorn, a scrubby tree, sand and stone – there's nothing to differentiate it from the surrounding desert.

There are no churches in Doha and no priests either, but an Anglican priest has flown in from another Gulf state to conduct the service. Forty friends, all young people, stand around the grave and join together in prayer. We have no music; no hymns nor flowers.

A few days after the service my friend has to leave the country. A young Englishman lies alone in a foreign land, buried in barren, stony ground.

The Sheik

We spent four Christmases in Qatar and on each we received a visit from a sheik. Warned ahead, we watched his Mercedes draw up at our gate and a chauffeur rush out to open the door. Then with gold-edged robe billowing out behind him like a spinnaker, the Sheik strode up the steps and came inside to offer us the season's greetings.

Once seated in our spartanly furnished living room he exchanged pleasantries with my husband, while I darted into the kitchen to pour out glasses of orange juice and open the chocolate biscuits I'd been told he favoured. He never stayed long, but before he left he always presented me with a gift, which was invariably a piece of gold jewellery.

My husband knew the Sheik because his company was involved in the same sewerage project, but the first year this happened we were thrown into confusion and I wondered whether I should accept his gift. But this was Arabia, and we had to consider the consequent loss of face involved if I didn't. The mere thought of it was daunting.

So that's how I became the owner of several hefty twenty-two-carat-gold bracelets, as well as necklaces and brooches studded with the local seed pearls.

MAURITIUS

House hunting

The agent has given us a map but we are having trouble finding the place. We drive up and down the road twice before we spot the gate, half hidden under a towering hedge of bougainvillea. As usual we're house hunting at the end of the day after my husband has finished work. It's already dark. There was a shower earlier, and the air is heavy with the scent of moisture pooling on tropical vegetation.

I open the gate and as we walk to the front door, the night fills with the sound of our feet crunching on the gravel path. Clouds hide the moon and we fumble around in the blackness of the porch, searching for the bell.

Before we can find it the door opens, temporarily blinding us with light. In stumbling French my husband asks the grizzled old man in front of us whether it's correct his house is available to rent.

'*Non, non!*' He shakes his head and waves us away.

'*Pardon,*' I say, and turn back towards the gate.

It's then I discover our second mistake. Giant snails completely cover what we thought was a gravel path – apart from the swathe of slimy destruction we wrought on our way to the front door.

Tortoise

Until we can find a suitable house to rent we stay in a hotel in Quatres Bornes, a town halfway up the mountain. On weekends we explore the island, which is beautiful beyond imagining. We drive through mountains and jungle and go with friends to see the giant water lilies growing in Pamplemousses Gardens.

No doubt there are other, equally gorgeous places where lagoons are edged by pristine beaches and multi-coloured shells lie in profusion on the warm white sand, but I haven't seen them.

We're walking along a narrow path near the beach when I hear twigs breaking and the sound of an animal crashing through the vegetation. Angus gives a cry and points to where a strange, primeval head pokes out at us from between two palm trees. A giant tortoise lumbers into the clearing. It stops, stares at us with round black eyes, then crosses the path and disappears in the jungle.

Manti

It's a month before we find a suitable place to rent. A wooden, ranch-style house, it's one of several donated by Western governments after a cyclone tore the island apart. We're to live in Moka, an agricultural area on the central plateau, where my husband is designing an irrigation system for the sugar plantations.

We've been in the house for an hour when I hear a sound, and looking through the window, see an Indian woman with a thick plait of hair reaching to the waist of her scarlet sari. I open the door and she turns toward me revealing a broad face – which, though not unpleasant, couldn't be described as beautiful.

'I'm Manti,' she says. 'I'm your maid.'

'I think you have the wrong house,' I tell her. 'I haven't advertised for anyone.'

In excellent English she makes it clear that she expects to be employed nevertheless.

'Come and see, Madame,' she says, and leads me across the lawn and down to the bottom of the garden, where a concrete hut is half hidden by the bamboo hedge. A small boy runs out of the door and buries his head between her legs.

'My home,' she says. 'And this is my son. I have no husband.' Then she looks at me.

It seems I have no choice. Clearly Manti comes with the house.

She starts work the following day. I quickly discover that she's far more capable than the young men we employed in the Gulf. They only swept the floors and cleaned the bathroom, but Manti understands our Western ways and immediately sets about making beds, emptying bins and loading the washing machine. I offer her a long-handled brush bought from the Chinese shop down the road, but she rejects it in favour of one already in the kitchen cupboard. It's a primitive thing, a witch's broom made of braided twigs.

Once she's finished sweeping Manti opens a tin of the red Cardinal polish used on floors all over the island. She slips a coconut husk under her foot. Then with rapid gyrations of her ankle she works her way across the floor, producing a brilliant shine without ever having to bend down.

Although I've had servants before, their presence in my home still makes me uncomfortable. In the first days of Manti's employment I shut myself in the bedroom while she cleans the living area, and we maintain a polite distance. Yet perhaps because of her pleasant, easy manner, it's not long before I find myself turning to her for advice and discover she's a mine of information on all aspects of island life.

Manti's a reliable worker too, and gives me no cause for complaint. But then one morning I spot my son's mug lying in pieces among the rubbish in the kitchen bin. Manti must have broken it when she was washing up. Angus loved that little mug with its nursery scenes and rabbits chasing each other around the rim. It was a present from his grandmother. It's Royal Doulton and I know I can't buy another in Mauritius. I'm cross – not because Manti has had an accident, but because she didn't tell me about it. I've begun to trust her, and this feels like deceit.

I find her in the garden, picking bananas.

'Why didn't you tell me when you broke Angus's mug?' I ask.

She looks puzzled. 'But, Madame,' she says, 'you are so rich. Why would you care about one small cup?'

I'm about to tell her that I *do* care and that Angus will be upset, when I remember her barefooted children and the concrete hut that doesn't have electricity, and I change my mind.

Most days Manti cleans while I cook our lunch, and we eat together. It's almost always the same – a simple curry of eggplant or the canned tuna she loves so much. Occasionally we have a piece of octopus caught by her brother who is a fisherman. The thick, leathery tentacles have suckers so massive that I can only guess at the creature's size.

Manti insists that we use fresh spices, so each morning we walk together to the market to buy turmeric and chili, coriander and cloves, cinnamon, cumin and star anise. Wherever I go I'm overwhelmed by the island's lush beauty. Everything grows easily here. Waterfalls of bougainvillea cascade over walls, avocados are twice the normal size, and within days of being erected, wooden fences sprout leaves.

We skirt around the rum-drunks lying unconscious on the pavement near the bus stop and turn into a small laneway. There we're overtaken by a gaggle of pigtailed girls snacking on green chilies as they walk to school. At the market the stallholder drops our spices into seven small newspaper cones, and we return home to grind them on the pillar of volcanic rock standing outside the kitchen door.

A carripoulé tree grows beside it. Manti plucks off a few of the dark, shiny leaves, and after adding them to the turmeric and other spices, sprinkles everything with water. Then she picks up the stone rolling pin and starts work.

In a minute she stops and turns around. 'You try,' she says.

And soon I'm yellow to the elbows.

The last Saturday in January is Thaipusam Cavadee. Manti invites me to accompany her to the celebration of this important Hindu festival. We set off around mid-morning and have gone a short distance when she veers off the road and enters the cane. Although it won't be harvested for a few months it's already tall enough to block our view, but we follow the sound of beating drums and soon come upon the procession. It's led by a man bearing a huge wooden arch adorned with ginger flowers, peacock feathers and palm leaves. Someone has driven a skewer through his tongue, and limes hang from the needles that pierce his chest. The next man drags a wheeled altar by chains and hooks clawed deep into his skin. He is followed by other penitents; some walking on nails, others tottering under the weight of

their wooden yokes. All are heavily pierced and yet strangely I see no blood nor sign of pain. The men whirl to the beat of the drums and one, trance-like, lurches across the path toward me. Afraid, I press my body hard against the cane.

The procession moves on, and I watch it slowly climb toward a white temple perched on the flank of the hill. Manti tells me offerings will be made there and milk poured over the statues.

One morning I find Manti in the bathroom, crying. When I ask what's wrong, she tells me her little daughter is well past the age when she should be walking, but as yet she can't even stand. She's been examined and had tests done at the hospital, but no explanation has been found. And now, Manti tells me, the doctors have warned her that the child may never walk.

I comfort her as best I can, and being English, offer her a cup of hot sweet tea. After we've talked for a while she seems to brighten and says suddenly, 'If the doctors can't help her, I have to make her well myself.'

The following morning Manti is late for work. She tells me it's because she's been to pray for her daughter in the Hindu temple, the Buddhist temple and both the Catholic and the Anglican churches. I look at her pityingly, but say nothing.

Two weeks later Manti bursts into the kitchen with the wonderful news that her daughter has taken her first steps. She's overjoyed. Now, she tells me, there's one small problem. Her prayers have been answered – but by which god?

She goes off to buy fruit and takes her offerings to the Hindu temple, the Buddhist temple, the Catholic church and, to be on the safe side, the Anglican church too.

Dark practices

Jane's a sensible woman with strong arms and broad shoulders, yet there's a softness about her, shown in the fleeting blushes that regularly cross her fair skin, and in the way she fusses over her two young daughters. Perhaps in England I wouldn't have sought out her company, but in Mauritius where I don't know anyone, I'm glad to have her as a friend.

Our husbands work together. We arrived at the same time, found houses, and both hired maids. I chose Manti – or rather she chose me. Jane's maid is of African descent; tall, stately, with skin the colour of ripe chestnuts.

Because she's expecting a baby, Jane won't see out the year in Mauritius; in a few months she'll return to England for the birth. She hasn't been well and she goes to bed in the afternoons, so it's fortunate she's found a person as capable as Désirée. I met the woman when I was at Jane's and I was impressed. She strides through the house organising meals, clearing up and generally taking care of Anna, who is three, and six-year-old Lucy. The girls seem fascinated by her.

Lately though I've noticed that when my friend mentions Désirée there's a certain hesitation in her voice, and I've begun to wonder whether something has happened. I know Jane's pregnant and has had a few health issues, but she seems listless and isn't the cheerful person I first knew.

We're sitting together by the pool one afternoon when I happen to glance across and catch her wiping away a tear.

'What is it?'

She looks uncomfortable. After moment she says, 'It's Désirée.'

'Désirée? But I thought you liked her? I've seen how good she is with the girls. They adore her.'

'That's the problem. I know it sounds silly, but lately I've had this feeling that she's trying to take over.'

'What do you mean?'

'If they need something they don't ask me anymore, they ask Désirée. They want *her* to dress them, want *her* to fix their hair. She puts in all those little braids that I couldn't possibly manage.'

'But she's a servant. They're *your* children. Why don't you tell her you want to take care of those things yourself?'

Jane looks confused. 'I've tried, but she doesn't take any notice of me. And there's a coldness in her voice that makes me nervous.'

I can tell from the look on her face that Jane has lost trust in the woman – that she's actually afraid of her.

'I think it's time to put a stop to this. Why don't you sack her and find someone who'll do as you say?'

She looks me in the eye. 'You're right. The next time she comes between me and the girls I'm going to remind her that they are *my* children. And maybe then I'll get rid of her.'

When we meet again, Jane looks radiant.

Before I can ask her why, she announces, 'I did it! I sacked her. Mind you, I was terrified. I didn't know what she might do.'

'How did you go about it?'

'I met her at the door and told her I didn't need her any longer. Then I gave her what I owed her. She smiled and walked away – it was easy.'

I can see the relief in her face. I tell her I'm sure she's made the right decision and that I'll ask Manti if she can find a suitable replacement.

'Don't do that,' Jane says. 'I've gone back to looking after the girls and doing the housework myself, and I'm enjoying it. I've felt much better since she left.'

I'm pleased to see her so happy, and I'm glad her problem has been resolved.

It's a while before I see Jane again. When I do, she's a wreck.

She tells me how the previous day she had answered a knock on her door and found Désirée standing there.

'She pointed her finger at my stomach,' Jane says. 'She was swaying from side to side and started this awful chanting. It was horrible. She's put a curse on my baby!'

I'm appalled, but try not to show it. 'This is primitive nonsense,' I tell her firmly. 'Don't take any notice of the silly woman. She's gone now. She can't hurt you.'

Jane nods, but I can see she doesn't believe me. I understand why she's so upset. I'm expecting a baby too, and like most women, hope and pray that my child will be normal.

We don't live in a leafy Hampshire suburb where this could be easily brushed aside as superstitious nonsense. Mauritius is gorgeous, but beneath its beauty lurks something dark and incomprehensible. The beaches are a paradise for tourists but up here in the wet centre, purple clouds hang like blankets over our heads and the island seems dark and forbidding. We've both seen candles flickering in the cemetery at night.

Since Désirée placed a curse on her, Jane has been back to her doctor to be thoroughly examined. He's reassured her there's nothing

wrong with her baby, but she doesn't believe him. She's becoming increasingly anxious and now she isn't eating properly, so I'm afraid Désirée may yet succeed in harming Jane's child.

In September Jane flies home to England. Sometime later I hear that she's given birth and, as it happens, her baby is fine. It's mine that has the problem.

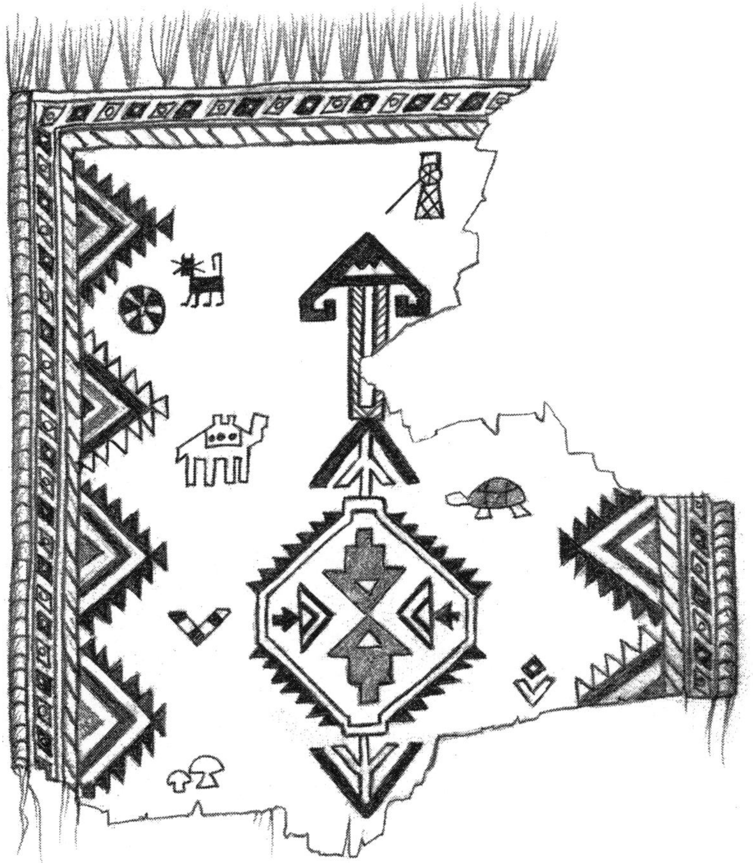

BROOK HOUSE

Brook House

We decide to buy a house in England because we need somewhere to stay when we're on annual leave, and also because there's often a gap of several months between the end of one overseas contract and the start of another.

We begin our search in the Lake District and eventually settle on a place in Crosby Ravensworth, a Cumbrian village of meandering lanes, centuries-old dry-stone walls and upland pastures.

Once part dwelling, part wheelwright's shop, the house we choose has a slate roof, brass latches on the doors and ceiling beams I can touch without standing on my toes. There's a date etched into the glass of an upstairs window – 1878. I run my fingers over the names of the family's eight children written below it and wonder how they all fitted into the house, which at that time, had only two small bedrooms.

My husband secures a contract in Abu Dhabi but it will be several months before he flies out. Meanwhile Angus attends the local primary school, and while he's away from home, we explore the village and climb the fells.

Cobnuts and blackberries grow among the hedgerows, and mushrooms in the meadows. In the early mornings we walk through fields wet with dew and bring home baskets filled with the snow-white cups, ready to be cooked for breakfast.

There are banks of stinging nettles beside the stream and my old friend Christine, who lives a few miles away, shows me how to cook them. Nicer than spinach, they are tasty and only slightly prickly on the tongue.

The old Rayburn in the kitchen heats both the water and the house. The oven is ideal for slow cooking but if the fire goes out it's almost impossible to re-light it. With that in mind, we gather kindling on the fell and use homemade 'paper sticks' to keep it burning.

Behind the house there's a field where farmers train their border collies and where sometimes visitors come to watch the sheep-dog trials.

Walking through the village one day we stop to speak to an elderly lady who is standing by her gate. She invites us into her cottage to try her parsnip wine. It seems innocuous, but after two small glasses I struggle to make it home.

Granny's visit

My mother-in-law has come to stay. She's a wonderful grandmother. She adores her grandchildren and believes it her solemn duty to indulge them at every opportunity. Since she only gets to see Angus when we return to England on annual leave, she concentrates her treats into short blocks, known in the family as 'Granny's Spoiling Weeks'.

They mostly take the form of shopping trips from which Angus returns chocolate-smeared and naughty. He easily persuades his grandmother to purchase the sort of gift that we, his parents, would only give for Christmas. She buys the biggest and the best: an oversized racing car, a speedboat too large to navigate the stream that flows past our garden, a plane connected by wires to a hand-held control box.

'Do you think that's suitable for a six-year-old?' I ask.

'There was a bigger one,' she says wistfully, 'but the shopkeeper wouldn't sell it to us. He said it might lift Angus into the air.'

It's Guy Fawkes Night, an occasion that lifts English spirits when frost patterns the windows, the last leaves have dropped from the trees and darkness falls too soon. I make gingerbread, and parkin from oats and black treacle, and Angus helps me thread toffee apples onto sticks. His father takes him into Penrith to buy fireworks: chrysanthemum fountains, snowstorms, jumping jacks and Catherine wheels. Angus persuades his grandmother to buy him a rocket. Naturally, it's enormous. In the evening we light a bonfire, and when it's dark we stand around it warming our hands on roasted chestnuts and slightly burnt potatoes. Angus twirls sparklers in flaming circles and my husband sets off a few fireworks. Then he turns his attention to the rocket. After pushing its wooden tail into our soggy lawn he cries, 'Stand back!' and lights the fuse.

We wait. Nothing happens.

'Light it again, Daddy,' says Angus moving forward, but I catch his arm.

There's a thunderous explosion followed by billowing, acrid smoke that leaves us choking and blind. When it clears a little I make out the shapes of my husband, my son and my mother-in-law, relieved to see they're all still upright. Angus tries to speak to me but there's something wrong with my ears and I can't hear him.

In the morning we go outside to look at the remains of our bonfire and see whether there's anything left of the rocket. But there's no sign of it – apart from the yawning crater in our front lawn.

Expecting – the unexpected

I glance at my watch and realise I must have fallen asleep in my chair. No wonder. Throwing a party for fifteen boisterous little boys has to be hard work at the best of times, but when you're heavily pregnant it's exhausting.

I get up to turn off the television but before I can reach it, I feel something warm running down my legs. I know at once what it is – my waters have broken. I study the widening pool on the floor, trying to come to terms with the inevitable. I'm having a baby. Not in five weeks when it's due, or even in two, when my husband will be coming home from the Gulf, but right now.

I'm excited, knowing the long wait is over, but my feelings are mixed with guilt. I've skipped those important, final weeks when my baby would have matured and reached a healthy weight.

It's midnight and I have a seven-year-old asleep upstairs. My friends and relatives live miles away, and we're not on the telephone. I check on Angus, then pull on my coat and hurry around to the pub next door.

The owner, a tough, no-nonsense widow in her late fifties, must still be awake because she answers my knock immediately. When I tell her why I need to use her phone, she hustles me inside and sits me down on an old-fashioned chamber pot so I don't drip all over her floor. Then she calls an ambulance. By the time it arrives Angus is safely tucked up in her spare bed.

My pains are coming every two minutes. The maternity hospital is a good three quarters of an hour away. And it's foggy. The ambulance officers crack jokes and jolly me along, but I catch their worried looks.

We make it to the hospital in time and I'm ushered into the delivery room ahead of half a dozen other women who've been in labour for hours. Within minutes, with a lusty cry, my baby is born.

'Is he all right?' I ask, when I'm told I have a son.

By way of answer, the midwife lays him in my arms. He's a dainty, fair-skinned, tiny soul. I count fingers and toes – he's perfect in every way. I hold him briefly before the midwife whisks him away to the warmth of an incubator.

I tell her then of my horrific experience following the birth of my first baby, and how terrified I am of being stitched. She sends for a gentle, kindly doctor who injects me with local anaesthetic so I don't feel a thing.

I came here alone, but in this little country hospital I feel surrounded by friends. In a few minutes a nurse wheels me into a single room and helps me into a warm bed where I fall asleep at once.

Christine

'There's someone here to see you,' whispers the midwife. 'She says her name's Christine.' She strokes the back of my hand. 'You don't have to see anyone if you'd rather not. I can send her away.'

'No, she's an old friend. Let her in.'

In true Christine fashion, she bursts into the room, words of congratulation bubbling from her lips. She moves toward the bed, but then takes in the expression on my face. Yellow roses wrapped in cellophane fall forgotten onto the coverlet. Immediately I'm sorry. Someone should have warned her.

'What is it?' she asks.

'He's not here. They've taken him away.'

I tell her about my recent conversation with the paediatrician called in from the hospital in Lancaster. About the pictures he drew to help explain what was wrong with my son, that child so beautiful and, in my eyes, perfect.

'I can't feed him,' I tell Christine. 'If I did, he'd drown. His oesophagus runs into his lung instead of his stomach. Even swallowing his own saliva could kill him.'

I see the tears welling in my friend's eyes and I feel guilty again. Someone should have prepared her for this.

'Where is he now?' she asks.

'In an ambulance on his way to Manchester. They took him to Lancaster first and they would have operated there if the problem was less complicated. They've told me he might not live.'

'Are you going to see him?'

'They won't let me out of here until tomorrow, and they say there's no point in rushing down there because I can't feed him. He's in mist, in an incubator. I can't even hold him.'

Christine sits down on the bed. She wraps her arms around me, and for the first time, I cry.

I'm discharged the following day. As I walk up the path to Brook House I'm hit by the strangeness of it all. I've had a baby, but I'm coming home alone.

The door opens, and there is my mother. My husband's plane is temporarily stranded in Saudi Arabia with engine failure, and he won't be home for another day or two. She's come to care for me in the meantime.

And so it begins – a journey between five distant hospitals, where Nathaniel will require intensive care and have two dozen operations, some minor and some life threatening.

Christmas

Someone has painted Disney characters on the glass along the corridor. Strings of coloured stars hang down from the ceiling, and my spirits lift at the sight of the Christmas tree beside the nurses' station – but only for a moment. It isn't the time for ward rounds, but ahead of me I can see a group of doctors and nurses standing around Nat's cot. My stomach lurches. I hurry over and squeeze between the white coats to get to him.

I've never seen anything like it. There's a huge swelling on my son's forehead – a hideous black bubble. My legs weaken and I grip the cot's rails, struggling to make the connection between this strange apparition and his current illness, his chest infection.

'What is it?'

Everyone turns to look at me and at once a nurse takes hold of my arm and ushers me away. 'Matron is waiting to speak to you.'

She leads me down a corridor and into her office. I've seen Matron when she made a rare visit to the ward, followed by a trail of fawning nurses. She's like God in this hospital. She doesn't usually bother with parents.

'Please sit,' she says curtly, adjusting her prim-starched bonnet. 'I have to tell you there was an unfortunate incident this afternoon, when your son was being weighed.'

I look at her stupidly. Nat is put on the scales every week. They are wheeled around the ward on a trolley and are at least chest-height above the marble floor.

'Unfortunately his nurse dropped one of the weights and when she bent down to look for it your son rolled off the scales and onto the floor. The poor girl! Can you imagine? She was so upset I had to give her the afternoon off.'

Hot blood rises in my veins. I open my mouth to tell her what *I* think of the poor girl, but she cuts me short.

There's ice in her voice. 'Your child is seriously ill, and I understand the only doctor prepared to operate on him attends in this hospital. I imagine you'd like his treatment to continue. You do understand what I'm saying, don't you?'

I understand. I know a threat when I hear one.

Back on the ward I ask whether Nat might have brain damage. The doctor says it's too soon to tell. Meanwhile the infection in his chest is raging, and when I use the catheter to clear his throat it fills with thick green mucus.

In the evening we're visited by a doctor wearing a turban.

'Is Nat going to get over this?' I ask him.

He smiles, then looks upward and raises his arms towards the ceiling. 'If God wills,' he says. 'It's in his hands now.' He smiles at me, then continues down the ward.

I pull my chair closer to Nat's cot and sit staring at the awful lump on his forehead. I'm cross. I didn't ask about God. I asked for a medical assessment. But surprisingly as the hours pass, I fill with gratitude for that Sikh doctor who, when I was lonely and afraid, shared with me his faith and humanity.

I haven't seen Angus in weeks. His father is working in Abu Dhabi, and he's been staying with his grandmother in Yorkshire since his brother was transferred to the London hospital. I've promised to be with him at Christmas, even if I can only stay for one night – long enough to give him his presents and watch him open his stocking.

I check the railway timetable and discover that because of the holiday there are only a few trains running. If Nat's condition worsens while I'm away I may not make it back to him in time. I can't take the risk. I go down to the lobby and call Angus to tell him I won't be with him on Christmas Day.

Moving house

It's February and bitterly cold in the north of England, where life exists in a murky twilight. At half past three, schoolchildren pass my gate and hurry home in the dark, and I've had the light on in my flat all day.

It's turned out to be a good place to rent, on the ground floor of this solid old house with its marble fireplace and fancy ceilings. When I first moved in, the flowerbeds were filled with crocuses and daffodils, and from my room I could see a mass of delicate pink blossom on the ornamental cherry tree in the middle of the lawn. But now in the darkness, sleeting rain hammers the windowpanes, rattling the glass and flowing down it in icy rivulets.

I move my chair nearer to the fireplace and throw on another shovelful of coal. The house is built of York stone and the cold has soaked deep into the chiselled blocks, blackened over the years by smoke from the woollen mill's chimney. The high ceiling and the cold draught that creeps around the door make it almost impossible to keep the place warm, but I'm doing my best for his sake.

I glance across the room to where he lies in his cot and I hear the familiar rattle in his throat. But then it clears, and he drifts back into his dream. It's a month now since his first birthday; three weeks since I brought him home from hospital – on the day I thought might never come. I carried him outside and when a gentle breeze ruffled his fine blond hair he cried out in fear, reminding me of how little he knew of the world.

He's an elfin child with a magical smile. He was a magnet to the well-meaning cleaners and visitors on his ward who cuddled him, breathed on him, and unwittingly harmed him. Because of the tracheotomy, his

breath isn't filtered by his nasal passages and has at times carried with it infections that have nearly killed him. It was time to bring him home.

He stirs, and I hear the bubbling of mucus rising in his throat. I hurry over to his cot, slip a rubber catheter into the hole under his chin and using suction from the rubber foot pump, clear his airway. Then calm again, he rolls over and falls asleep almost immediately. We'll be repeating the process four or five times during the night because I can't risk a blockage in that little tube.

I've made my decision, and in a week we'll be gone. It's months now since Angus joined my husband in Abu Dhabi, and they've waited long enough. Of course the doctors told me Nat should stay in hospital. They said babies like mine need constant supervision, and when I told them where I was taking him they were shocked.

'Why would you fly a sick child to a Third World country with primitive medical facilities?' they asked.

But with all their sophisticated equipment they can't cure him. And it's time for him to start living.

I step out of the plane into the warm night air and the intoxicating smell of the desert. My husband is waiting with Angus on the edge of the airstrip. They call out to me and embrace Nathaniel, this golden child they haven't seen for so long.

We drive through the darkness, chattering endlessly. There's so much to tell, so much to share. By the time we reach the flat both boys are exhausted and I soon have them tucked into bed. Amid the joy of having my family together again, the anxiety and stress of the past months slip away. I take off my jacket and thick woollen jumper and put on a flimsy slip. I reach out to my husband and we soon drift off to sleep.

Sometime later I'm awakened by the *muezzin* calling the faithful to prayer. For a while the pleasant, rhythmic sound echoes around my head. Then in a panic I realise it is morning and I haven't cleared Nat's airway all night. I throw myself out of bed and rush to his room, dreading what I might find.

He's sitting up in his cot playing with a little red car. As I come through the door he holds out his arms to me. A shaft of light illuminates his face, and for the first time I see a healthy glow in his cheeks.

STARS IN THE SEA

Stars in the sea, stars in the sky

At dusk we go down to the beach and spread out our rugs on the sand. There's a crowd of us; families with children and a few young, single engineers who all work for the same company. While the men gather driftwood, we women thread pineapple and capsicum, steak, onion and tomato onto skewers, ready to be grilled over the fire.

We feed the children first, then lay out their bedding on the beach and settle them down to sleep under the stars. So many stars, and a moon that glows above us like a great silver beacon. It's August, the middle of summer and the sun is our enemy, the moon our friend. When we see it rise in the sky we know that life outdoors has become bearable again.

One evening we wait for the children to go to sleep, and then wade into the shallows in darkness before the moon has risen. It's when I disturb the water with my hand that I first see them – a thousand pinpricks of light glittering on my skin. Friends call out to each other in delight, and as we scoop up handfuls of the tiny plankton, the sea around us shines with life.

At a party I'm introduced to our neighbor who is a professional diver. He has the use of an inflatable, a Zodiac, and he offers to take me and my girlfriend diving. It's too good an opportunity to miss, so the following day the three of us meet at the beach for a basic lesson in how to stay alive underwater.

Then it's time for the dive. I encourage my friend to go first. I can swim breaststroke, but not the crawl because I don't like dipping my face into the water. When it's my turn, I'm nervous.

David holds my hand as we drop ten metres to the reef below. Shoals of brilliantly coloured fish swim around me and peer into my mask. Ferocious-looking moray eels poke out their heads from crevices. Striped sea snakes weave between the corals searching for food, but in this magical garden so full of beauty I forget to be frightened.

In the following weeks we three meet regularly at the beach, and I look forward to putting on my diving gear and helping to launch the Zodiac. One day three good-sized sharks swim for a while behind the boat, apparently attracted by the sound of its engine.

'What do you do if you see a shark when you're diving on the reef?' I ask Dave.

'With luck I'll have my underwater camera with me,' he says, 'and I can get some good pictures.'

His attitude toward sharks doesn't surprise me. Half-man, half-fish, he glides through the water with such sure calm that when I'm with him I, too, am unafraid.

Then a new movie arrives in Abu Dhabi. It's called *Jaws.* I go to see it with friends who also enjoy scuba diving. We emerge from the cinema changed people.

There's a sudden rush to buy broom handles and nails to make the 'billies' Jacques Cousteau recommends for warding off sharks. At the end of a hot day we still go down to the beach, but we remember those nighttime shots of dangling legs, taken from a shark's-eye view. The relentlessly threatening da-da-da-da of the theme music rattles around in our heads and we stay out of the water once it's dark.

I dive one last time. The beauty of the reef is lost to me now. I'm forever staring into the distance, searching for a pointed nose or a sudden flick of a tail.

Shark attacks are rare, and the risk to a diver is small. I know that, but it doesn't help. If I see one I suspect I'll throw off my weight belt and shoot straight to the surface, causing a bubble of gas to form in my bloodstream.

It won't be the shark that kills me, it'll be my fear.

The tube

We're in the hospital again for yet another attempt at taking out Nat's tracheotomy tube. This is the third time he and I have flown back from the Gulf, the third time I've prayed for a miracle.

It's not that Nat is unhappy or unwell or that caring for him is difficult. Though in truth when I first brought him home I was terrified, knowing his life depended on my being able to keep his tube clear. What if it becomes blocked during the night while I'm asleep? What if, when I'm replacing the tube, the hole under his chin closes over and I can't push in the new one?

But since then I've grown confident. I cope with his frequent chest infections and I manage his other problems as they arise. My trusty little foot pump is always with me, ready to clear Nat's airway whenever and wherever it's needed – down the street, in the car or on an aeroplane.

Once I even used it in the public library. A woman walked around the row of shelves, book in hand, took one look at what I was doing and panicked. I had a hard time dissuading her from calling an ambulance. But our friends in Abu Dhabi are accustomed to seeing me crouched over my son, catheter in hand, and it doesn't bother them at all.

Nat's healthy now; there's colour in his cheeks and he's putting on weight. He can paint a picture, build a Lego car and fasten his own shoes. He'd be like any other little boy if it weren't for the way he breathes and, of course, the fact he's three years old and I've never heard him speak.

The surgeon comes to see us. He tells me that as usual Nat will be anaesthetised before he takes out the tube. Then he'll wait to see how long it will be before his throat collapses again and the attempt has to be abandoned. That took two minutes last time.

'No more anaesthetics,' I say. 'Nat doesn't breathe as strongly when he's asleep.'

'But if we take out the tube while he's awake he'll panic, and that'll be the end of it,' the doctor says.

He may well be right, but I've thought about it carefully and I'm determined. 'This time I'll take it out myself,' I say. 'But not in theatre. On the ward, with no doctors or nurses around.'

He looks at me doubtfully, but he doesn't argue. He knows he hasn't had any luck trying it his way.

I go shopping, and mid-afternoon return to the ward with a box of Lego under my arm. There's a pair of round-ended scissors ready for me on top of Nat's locker. I lift him onto my knee, then casually snip the tapes from around his neck.

As he reaches for the Lego I pull out his tube. A horrible, rasping sound emerges from his throat but then he breathes – through his nose. Absorbed in studying the picture on the front of the box, he's oblivious to the fact that something momentous has happened.

I pull off the sticky tape, lift out the plastic envelope of coloured bricks and we start to build a fire engine. After a while I glance down at my watch. Five minutes! I study Nat's chest. He's breathing normally. I'm exultant. Even if the tube has to go back in immediately, we've made progress and I'm convinced now that one day he will be free of the thing.

Two nurses have been watching discreetly from the doorway, and they signal to me. 'Everything OK?'

I nod reassuringly.

Time passes. Nat eats, drinks his milk and shows no signs of discomfort. But now he's getting tired. I help him undress and prepare him for bed.

Sister comes to look at us and introduces me to the nurse who is to 'special' Nat throughout the night. She's Canadian, a temp sent in from an outside agency. She looks pleasant enough, but I haven't met her before and at a time like this it's hard to trust Nat's wellbeing to a total stranger.

I make sure she understands how much this means to me – this outside chance of my son leading a normal life. He requires constant supervision. As long as that tube is in his throat there'll be no going out alone, no bike rides with his friends, no playing in the garden out of my sight and no hope of attending school.

The nurse listens carefully; tells me she understands. 'But you need to know that if I think Nat is in serious trouble, the decision on whether to replace his tube or not will be mine, and mine alone,' she says.

Together we settle him down for the night, sitting on either side of the bed until he falls asleep. I look out of the window at the lights of the city below, thinking please God give him this chance, make it happen this time.

An hour passes; two. And then it begins. He stirs in his sleep, sits up, coughs. The cough grows louder, stronger. It racks his skinny body and turns his face vermillion. He struggles for breath and there's fear in his eyes. I glance up to see nurses rushing onto the ward, closely followed by the mother of a child whose room is at the far end of the corridor. All are looking for the source of this dreadful, desperate sound.

My Canadian nurse picks Nat up from the bed, tips him over her knee and pats his back repeatedly, loosening whatever it is that's blocking his airways. In a moment the coughing eases and his face returns to a more normal colour. She sits him up, calms him, gives him some oxygen. Then she props him up on his pillows, moving them this way and that until she's satisfied he's in the best position. In another five minutes he's asleep. The other nurses return to their duties and I breathe a sigh of relief.

And so it goes on. Over and over, all night long. An hour's sleep followed by a demonstration of nursing at its best, delivered by my wonderful Canadian temp. Several times she looks at me and shakes her head, but she perseveres and I can tell she isn't going to give up without a fight.

Then as I stare out of the window I see a pale glimmer on the horizon, and soon the streetlights and then those in the surrounding buildings are switched off. Despite our being so high above the city the increasing noise of traffic permeates the room.

I look down at my son and see that he's sleeping peacefully. His new life is about to begin.

On a Kuwaiti beach

We've driven a long way to reach this beach, a hot sticky drive in a car without air conditioning, and all for my sake. Near our home in Fahaheel there's a stretch of sand where Nat can play with a ball or splash around in the shallows with his father. It's a fine place for them, but not for me. I can't undress; my bikini would soon attract the unwanted attentions of migrant workers long denied the sight of a woman's flesh.

I have no wish to offend local sensibilities. I wear a long-sleeved, floor-length caftan when I'm shopping in Kuwait, and I don't go out alone. But marooned all week in an upstairs flat while my husband works, I long for the freedom of this deserted beach.

Now Nat runs off with his bucket and spade and I strip off my shirt and dive into the turquoise water. Later, made half stupid by the heat and the cloying perfume of coconut oil on my skin, I lie down under our umbrella. My muscles relax, the sun's glow permeates my eyelids and I drift in and out of a warm orange dream.

At the water's edge my husband, the engineer, is helping his son build a sandcastle town with moats, bridges and, quite possibly, a sewerage works. Every few minutes I raise myself onto my elbows to review their progress before I stretch out again.

My reverie is disturbed by voices speaking in Arabic and I see a man and two women walking across the sand toward me. I can tell they are Kuwaitis. He wears the traditional white *dishdasha* and headdress held in place by a circle of black cord. His companions' dark robes hide their bodies, and their faces are shielded by the beak-like masks commonly worn by women of the Gulf state.

Not wishing to embarrass them, I reach for a shirt to cover my exposed skin, but as the three pass by, the man deliberately looks away. Selecting a spot farther along the beach, he sets up chairs and an umbrella.

A few minutes later I see the women stand up and wade into the sea until the water reaches their thighs. They can't swim, I'm sure of that. Caught by the waves, the material of their *abayas* billows out around them and restricts their every move.

I wonder what they think of my willingness to expose bare arms, legs and midriff to public view. They must think me highly disrespectful of Allah – a harlot. I decide to ignore them. I lie down on my towel, close my eyes and allow the gentle breeze to dry the beads of perspiration on my skin.

My half-sleep is broken by the sound of footsteps and before I can cover myself again, one of the women is standing in front of me. I jump up to greet her. She holds out her hand, revealing a delicate flower perched on a hennaed palm. Each petal-like segment is so neatly cut that it's a moment before I realise I'm being offered an orange.

'*Shukran, shukran,*' I say, taking the fruit from her hands. I look past the strangeness of the mask and read her sweet smile in her eyes. And as she turns away, I hear her tinkling laughter.

Esrom

We're on leave in the Lake District, catching up on all the things we can't get in Kuwait. As it happens booze, although forbidden, isn't one of those. I make an excellent red wine (strictly for our own use) from packets of frozen blackberries and grape juice. Beer hasn't been a problem either, except for the night when thirty bottles exploded in the bathroom. I overdid the yeast.

Pork is banned, but there's 'breakfast bacon' made from beef. We can't get mushrooms in Kuwait but they grow wild in the fields behind Brook House.

Most of all we miss good cheese. There's a little shop in Penrith that has the best – not just the usual cheddar, red Leicester and sage Derby, but also Swaledale, stinking bishop – and esrom. A Danish cheese once made by monks, it's semi-soft with tiny holes and full of flavour. We're especially fond of it and plan to send a big slab back to Kuwait at the end of our leave.

The desert has its own beauty but I miss England's rich green landscape. I'd like to take a little of it with me, so a few days before our return I visit a nursery and buy two dozen indoor plants. After wrapping them in wet newspaper, I pack them into cardboard tubes ready to be sent by airfreight. I don't know whether they'll survive, but I can already imagine a glorious jungle growing at one end of my living room.

We put the slab of esrom in the bottom of the box, which we take with us when we go to the airport.

A day or so after our arrival in Kuwait my husband goes to collect it. At the shed where airfreight is stored, he's told that it hasn't arrived. The man doesn't know why. Aware that it could be in Iran, Pakistan or Oman by now, I assume that all my plants will be dead by the time they're found – if they are.

Two weeks pass, then suddenly there's a message to say that our box has turned up. Will we come to the airport to collect it? We arrive at the shed and show the official our documents.

His eyes glaze over. 'It's yours!' he says. *'Alhamdulillah!'*

He opens a door and we're almost knocked over by the smell – a cross between a pigsty and a hundred sweaty socks. Our esrom has matured.

We drive back with the car windows down. When we reach home I cut through the tape, take a deep breath and open the lid.

My plants are alive! Not only that – new leaves have grown. Some of the flowering plants are now in bud, and long green tendrils have wound themselves around the cardboard tubes. The heat and fetid humidity have worked a miracle and I shall have my lounge room jungle after all.

I gingerly lift out the esrom. It's still in one piece, but when I cut into it, the cheese collapses into a gelatinous mess with the consistency of old knicker elastic. We spread it on dry biscuits, taste it, and we're in heaven.

In the desert

'I'm hungry, is there anything to eat?'

I search through my bag for a biscuit, twist around and hand it to Nat in the back seat. 'You'll have to make do with this till we get home. Why didn't you sit down and eat a proper meal with everyone else?'

At lunchtime I offered him a lamb chop, steak and even cake, but he was more interested in climbing the sand dunes and searching for lizards with our friends' young son.

'Are you cold? Do you need a jumper?'

I pull on my own coat. Black, brown, white striped and billowing, it's like a Bedouin tent. I'm glad of its warmth. We've basked all day under a gentle winter sun but now it's low on the horizon and the desert is cooling. To our left rows of crescent-shaped dunes glow fiercely orange, and the two cars throw long shadows onto the vast gravel plain over which we're travelling. We're heading back to Fahaheel in the tyre marks of a hundred earlier cars.

Up ahead I see a man in a dark *dishdasha* and red-checked head cloth standing beside the track. He waves his arms, gesturing that we should stop. In a moment he's at the window, explaining how his vehicle has broken down. Can we give him a lift?

My husband signals his intentions to our friends in the car behind. The man gets in and points to where a lone date palm breaks the horizon. Soon after, we come upon his stranded family standing around a rusty old truck. The three men in our group get out and offer assistance. We have spare water for the radiator and a can of petrol in our boot, but a problem with the engine can't be easily fixed.

'Where are you heading?' asks David, our neighbour. He glances around at the dozen or so women and children and adds, 'Perhaps we can give some of you a lift?'

The man translates, faces brighten and the whole family converges on our already half-filled cars. Leaving the front to the father and his young son, I get in the back and put Nat onto my knee. A girl of four or five and two women, one with baby, squeeze in on either side.

Unlike other Kuwaiti women I've met, these are unveiled and appear relaxed and friendly even around our menfolk. They chatter to each other, smile at Nat and try by sign language to initiate conversation with me. One, who appears old enough to be a grandmother, wears a bracelet of hollow silver balls which rattle when she moves her hand. She has a series of blue dots tattooed across her chin in what must be a traditional, tribal pattern.

The second woman is mostly hidden from me by the children crushed between our bodies, but the patterned hem of her purple skirt lies against my ankle and I can see the embroidered cuffs of her pantaloons. We are nine, crammed together in what is an average-sized car. And yet it feels oddly exhilarating, this intimate confinement with strangers.

I assume the family has, like ours, spent a pleasant Friday picnicking in the desert and is returning home to the city or one of the coastal villages. So I'm surprised and a little unnerved when at

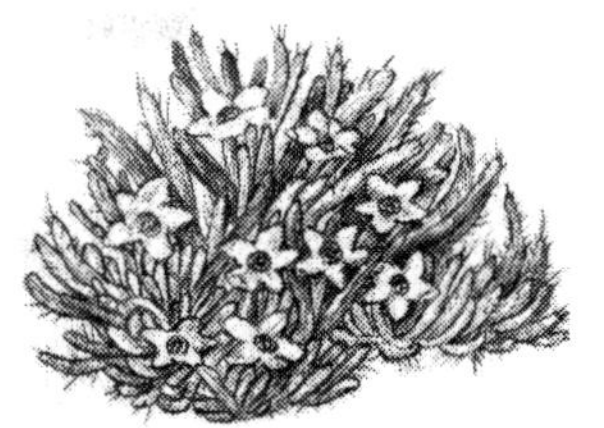

the father's instruction, my husband turns inland. For a while he follows a partially obliterated track and after that comes to an end, drives on across pale sand unmarked by footprint or tyre.

It's rained recently and we enter an area where tiny shrubs with yellow, daisy-like flowers have sprung up between sand and stone. In reality the emerging shoots are sparsely dotted across the desert's floor, but from a distance the shallow *wadis* appear as green as new mown lawn.

We go over a rise and I see a flock of goats and fat-tailed sheep spread out across the plain, and in the distance, the striped tents of the Bedouin. It's clear now; our passengers are not townsfolk but desert nomads. We let them out just short of the tents and then all get out to stretch our legs.

Before we can return to the cars we're mobbed by a crowd of curious children. They're joined by a group of young women and a second man, more portly than the first. It quickly becomes apparent that we won't be allowed to leave before partaking of the family's hospitality.

Rugs smelling of unwashed goat hair are spread out on the ground and we're invited to sit down. Wood smoke spirals from a nearby hearth where water is heating in a blackened pot. Two women emerge from a tent carrying strings of dates, and another invites us to drink directly from a bowl filled to the brim with buttermilk.

Weevils are crawling over the dates. As we eat, the busy little creatures jump off the fruit and run up our arms. The buttermilk is warm. Curds float in a sea of yellow fat. I recognise the generosity of our hosts, stifle back my revulsion, and drink.

Four boys, a few years older than Nat, appear from behind the tent, bringing with them a pair of lambs. I admire their soft white coats and long floppy ears hanging from little brown heads. A boy lays one in my lap. Obviously accustomed to being cuddled, it's unafraid and rests comfortably in my arms.

The Bedu love their animals. They are the family's wealth; their meat, their drink and their means of survival in a harsh land. The man to whom we gave a lift explains that these lambs are twins – rarely born to Awassi sheep. He tells me proudly that he owns a hundred sheep and goats.

Our friend Mark, the father of Nat's little friend, asks if he can take a photograph. To my surprise, despite there being unveiled women present, he is given permission and goes to collect his camera from the car. When he returns everyone crowds around, eager to be in the picture. There must be at least twenty family members in addition to the seven of us. We press together: English men, tribal women, Bedouin children and sheep.

The sun drops from the sky, the colours of the desert shift and a chill breeze ripples the sand. It's time to go home. I stand up and indicate to one of the boys that he should take back his lamb.

Before I can place it in his arms, his father steps between us and waves the boy away. Confused, I tell him we're leaving. He nods, smiles and points towards the car. Suddenly I understand – he's giving me a sheep. I try to explain that I can't accept such a valuable present. That I'm not equipped to care for it.

He turns his back on me and walks off in the direction of the tents. My husband gives me a warning look and I remember that I'm in Arabia, where the rejection of a gift can cause severe hurt and loss of face. I worry that I have offended our host, but soon he returns bringing with him a sack filled with grain.

'For the sheep,' he says, handing it to me.

I thank him for his kindness and for his family's hospitality, and carry the lamb to the car. Nat is delighted. He cuddles up to his woolly friend on the back seat and it isn't long before they are both sound asleep. We reach the main road as darkness falls.

'What are we going to do with this lamb?' I ask my husband.

But he's passed the day in the company of friends, enjoyed our picnic in the desert and met the Bedouin. He's in no mood to worry about one little sheep.

When we arrive home I carry it into the lift and take it up to our fourth floor flat with its cream carpet. Nat plays with the lamb and later takes it to bed with him. I mop up the puddles.

Next day I phone the Indian lady who babysits. When I offer her the lamb she accepts with alacrity and is round to collect it within the hour, and I don't dare ask what she intends to do with it.

Greece

Temperatures in Kuwait are in the high forties and frequent power cuts result in us spending the night in a paddling pool on the lounge-room floor. My husband, who has to stay behind for his work, generously suggests that Nat and I get on a plane and escape for a while.

A week later we're on the deck of a ferry carrying locals, visitors, furniture and goats to a Greek island in the middle of a navy-blue sea.

At the jetty we're met by a crowd of jostling women looking for tourists to put up in their homes. After I say 'yes' to the first one that accosts me, she leads us to the village's main square and up some steps to a whitewashed room above a café. It's clean, comfortable – and noisy.

We're tired. It's been a long trip and Nat soon falls asleep on his bed. But the racket from down below gets noticeably louder, and when I look out of the window I see two local women having an argument. In a minute they're punching each other. I expect someone to pull them apart. Instead the whole square erupts as their respective families, armed with the broken-off legs of the café's wooden chairs, join in the melee. Then as suddenly as it started, the battle ends and everyone goes home.

In the morning we move to quieter accommodation – a white stone hut some distance from the village, but within metres of the sea. We lie in bed at night listening to the waves lapping on the shore, and wake at sunrise to wander among hillsides scented with wild thyme. We discover windmills with flapping sails and tiny whitewashed churches with blue domes. We eat potatoes and herb-grilled chicken in the same café every day, and in the afternoons Nat builds sandcastles and elaborate harbours for his boats. He is content, and I have my book.

In two days I've read it. Now what? I don't have another. By the end of the week I think I'll go mad with boredom. But then a strange thing happens. My whole being slows, and in the stillness and silence of the evening I feel the beating of my heart. And I discover that to be truly content, all I need is a bed, a mat, a wooden chair and the sound of the sea.

Moving on

After working in Kuwait for three years, my husband is promoted to his company's head office in Athens.

A week after we arrive we receive our first invitation to visit a Greek home. We're already acquainted with our host who, like us, recently lived and worked in Kuwait. Even so, I'm a little nervous. My mastery of the Greek language extends to yes, no, thank you and – when I remember – goodbye. We haven't met his family and I'm not sure whether we are invited for dinner, drinks, or just coffee and a chat. I wonder what would be an appropriate gift to take along. In some countries visitors turn up with a bottle of wine or even a plate of food. In others that might be taken as a slur on the host's ability to cater adequately for his guests. Perhaps a bunch of flowers would be the safest option?

When we reach the house there are cars parked all over the front lawn and halfway down the street. Our friend greets us at the door and shows us into the living room where a birthday party is in full swing. We're surrounded by relatives and neighbours who vigorously shake our hands and then, pressing plates into them, urge us to eat, eat and eat.

Amid shouting and laughter children aged between two and twelve chase each other around tables piled high with seafood, moussaka and spanakopita. Recovering from his initial shyness, our five-year-old decides to join in and runs off to play with his new friends.

Plates are filled and refilled, the birthday cake is cut and then, as the party quietens somewhat, the menfolk retire to a room at the back of the house where a bar has been set up. With my husband gone, I find myself sitting among a group of stern-faced elderly aunts in long black dresses. They don't speak English and I don't speak Greek.

We attempt to communicate through mime.

One lady points at a little boy sitting nearby, then holds out her palm at different levels. I interpret that to mean 'How old are your children?'.

In reply I hold up my fingers to denote five and twelve.

'Boys or girls?' (At least I think that's what I'm being asked.)

I try to answer with a gesture that isn't rude.

'Why only two?'

That's a question to which I can't and won't reply. Instead I smile and shrug my shoulders. After a couple of minutes it all becomes too difficult and they give up and talk among themselves.

Then the children, who have been watching cartoons, are ushered out of the room and the door is closed. Our hostess loads a video into the machine and smiles at me encouragingly. Is this to be a film of her last holiday, meant to introduce me to Greece's ancient sites: its monasteries perched high on mountain tops, the clear blue seas, the white windmills of the Cyclades?

The buzz of conversation drops away as all eyes focus on the screen where, with the briefest nod at foreplay, a young couple rip off their clothes and commence a series of contortions involving all the orifices known to man.

Stunned, I sneak a glance at the austerely clad ladies with whom I earlier conversed, anticipating outraged cries and a flurry of skirts as they flounce out of the room. But after watching impassively for a few minutes they return to their knitting and chatter, leaving me with the strong impression that they've seen this movie at least once before.

And I'm the only one embarrassed.

A Greek Christmas

While my husband works, Nat and I explore the labyrinth of streets flanking the Acropolis and scramble in brilliant white light among its ancient stones.

We've already made enquiries about suitable schools and in the evenings go house hunting. Yet after a few weeks I become aware that something is wrong. My husband is unhappy.

'I don't like being stuck in an office all day,' he confesses, when I press him. 'I've always been a site engineer. I miss the outdoors.'

'If you don't like the job you should quit,' I say.

So he does. But before he can find another engineering position overseas, he'll have to return to the UK. That's where the jobs are advertised and where the interviews take place.

It's winter. We've heard reports of severe snowstorms in the north of England and I fear for Nat's health if we go there. Instead we arrange for Angus to join us in Greece as soon as the term ends at his boarding school, and we make plans to spend Christmas in the islands.

Without our usual turkey, crackers or decorations, it's a strange sort of celebration, but I boil up a fruitcake in lieu of plum pudding and on Christmas Day, Nat charms the locals by singing 'Little Donkey' in the local taverna.

When Nat and I first visited the islands the streets were filled with holidaymakers. There are no tourists now. The Aegean is the same brilliant blue but a fierce, unrelenting wind buffets the shore and whistles through the narrow laneways between the houses. It's cold and rainy. Our whitewashed cottage has no heating and the toilet is outdoors, on the roof. In the middle of the night I climb the stairs and step outside – into ankle-deep water.

Half-frozen, we scour the local shops for hot-water bottles and when we don't find any, carry stones up from the beach and boil them in a pan of water. They warm our beds and only sometimes, towards morning, wake us when they crash to the floor.

In the New Year we return to England and my husband applies for another position, this time in Singapore. The Lake District is colder than our beautiful Aegean island, but at least here we have thick blankets, real hot-water bottles and a wood fire to keep us warm.

SINGAPORE

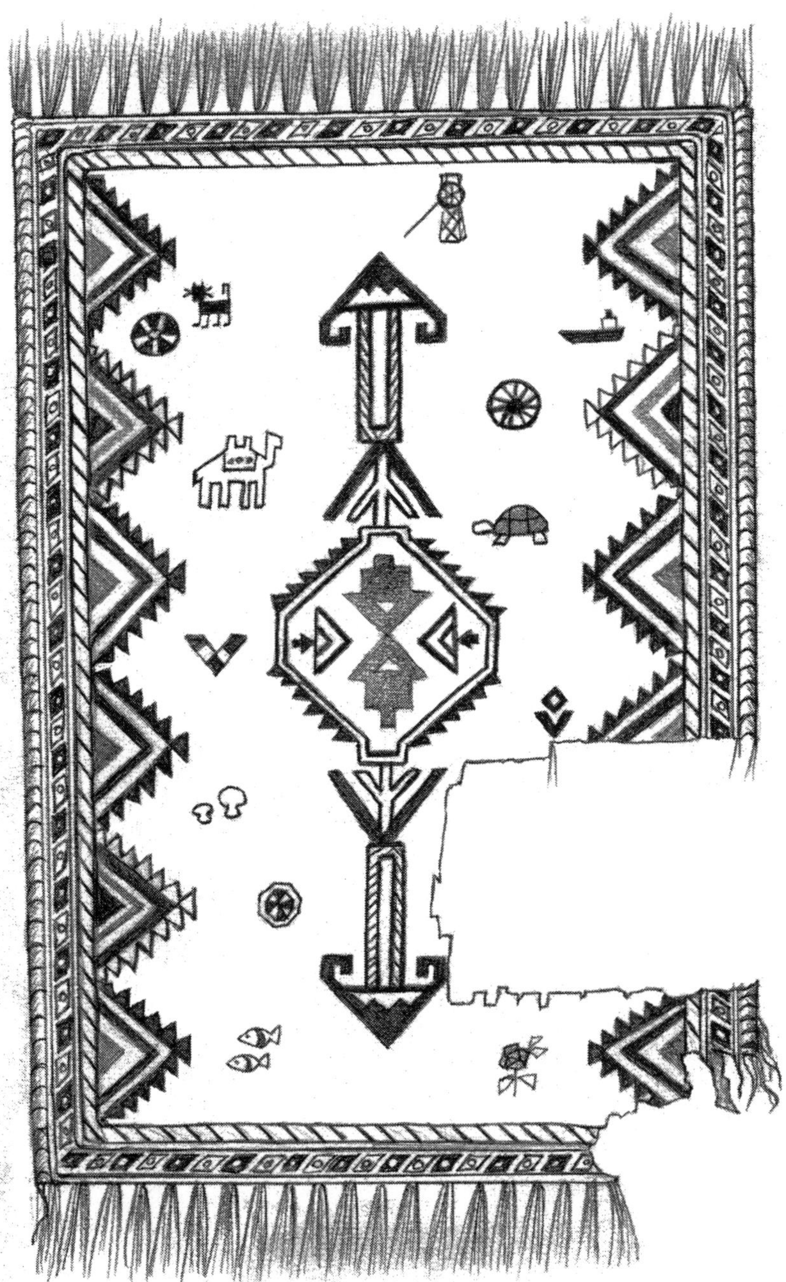

Singapore

Clouds of purple bougainvillea hang from the bridges on the freeway and tropical vegetation shades the city streets. Milk is delivered to my door, and after a night out with friends I can walk home alone without feeling nervous. I don't have to work on Christmas Day, Deepavali, Chinese New Year, Vesak Day, Hari Raya Haji, or at Easter. I can eat laksa whenever I like.

And I have a friend. She lives in the kampong at the bottom of our road. I met her after Nat fell off his bike into one of Singapore's deep roadside drains and she brought him home, cut and bleeding. Her name is Zubi. She's Muslim, she's Malay, and she has a gentle wisdom on which I rely when everything seems to be falling apart.

Laughed at

I'm hungry. I drive to Newton Circus and order a plate of green kangkong and three dollars' worth of cockles from one of the open-air hawker stalls. Then I sit at a table under a mango tree sipping juice from a fresh coconut, until the girl brings me an enormous pile of shells sitting in brown gravy.

I pick one up and try to open it. I can't. I try another. No. Perhaps they haven't been boiled for long enough? I'm about to give up and order something else, when I notice the locals at the next table watching me with interest. I decide I won't be beaten by a few shellfish. After several more attempts I find the right spot and succeed in prizing one open with my thumbnail. From then on it's plain sailing. The cockles have a pleasant, chewy texture and slightly fetid flavour.

A Chinese grandmother comes over to look at the English lady surrounded by shells and up to her elbows in gravy – and goes away laughing.

After I've eaten I walk back to my car, an old Triumph Spitfire with a convertible roof. I don't put it up very often. The rusted metal poles

have to be slotted into each other. The ageing canvas has shrunk and it's a struggle to stretch it over the frame.

I'm driving along Scotts Road in heavy traffic and am nearly at the corner of Orchard Road when I stop for a red light. As I do, there's a deafening thunderclap and lightning sizzles around me, making the little hairs on my forearms stand upright. Rain falls from the sky as if thrown from a bucket. Within seconds my shirt becomes transparent, and water, trapped inside the car, swirls around my ankles.

Above the sound of the rain I hear laughter and I look up to see that I'm surrounded by truck drivers waving and pointing at me. But being British I ignore them, look steadfastly to the front and wait for the lights to change.

News of a death

Barely six months after our arrival in Singapore, my mother calls to say that my father has died.

I haven't seen or spoken to him since we walked down the aisle together on my wedding day. My mother doesn't know it, but I'm in the throes of a divorce and if I'm honest with myself, right now I don't much care whether he's alive or dead. The news brings with it an end to all those years of disappointment and false hope. I tell her I'm sorry.

At the movies

On my tenth birthday my mother took me to see *Seven Brides for Seven Brothers*. Shortly before the end of the film, when the girls decided they were in love after all and would marry their kidnappers, a man put his hand on my knee.

I didn't push it away. I didn't cry out and I didn't say anything to my mother who was sitting right next to me. Instead I watched, mesmerised, as his fingers gently stroked my thigh and began creeping upwards.

Then the movie finished, the lights came on and the hand vanished.

'Are you ready to go?' asked my mother, reaching for her bag.

I stood up and followed her out into the aisle without so much as a glance at the man in the next seat.

'Did you enjoy the film?' she asked. 'Wonderful music wasn't it?'

I agreed, and we walked up Westgate and caught the 7.15 bus back home.

That night I lay in bed struggling to understand what had transpired in the cinema. It had made me feel dirty, and I knew I would never be able to tell anyone about it.

Twenty-seven years later I'm sitting alone in a cinema in Singapore when, halfway through the movie, a man puts his hand on my knee. I look down at the fingers resting on my skirt and for the second time in my life, make no attempt to push them away.

Summoning up my best British school-ma'am voice, I say loudly, 'Would you kindly remove your hand from my thigh?'

Everyone within earshot turns and gawks at my assailant who leaps to his feet, scrambles over the couple seated to his right and dashes for the exit. Unfazed by all the attention, and with a smile on my face, I settle back in my seat and thoroughly enjoy the rest of the movie.

Sri Lanka – Hikkaduwa beach

After a day spent sightseeing, my boyfriend and I go down to the beach and stretch out on the warm sand. The sun hovers briefly above an iridescent sea, and then falls below the horizon. Darkness comes swiftly and there's a rustling in the palm fronds above our heads as flocks of tiny birds select their perches and settle for the night.

A group of teenage boys in Nike T-shirts have lit a fire near the water's edge, and ribbons of wood smoke drift slowly across the beach towards us. One young man stands up, walks over to where we're lying and invites us to join his party.

His friends offer us cans of the local beer and the boys move over to make space for us beside their campfire. We're glad of its warmth. The temperature has dropped and there's a fresh breeze blowing off the sea.

As we sit and talk, our hosts become pleasantly drunk and the fire burns to a rosy glow. Here and there a tongue of yellow flame flickers among the lengths of driftwood and we back away from the heat, shuffling our bottoms in the sand.

The young man sitting beside me wants to hear about our trip. I describe our visit to the Temple of the Tooth in Kandy and then mention my disappointment at having missed a recent Tamil festival.

'I've been told that after believers have eaten particular foods and said special prayers they are able to walk on fire without burning their feet.'

The boy laughs. 'Anyone can do that,' he says. 'Watch!' He rips off his trainers and leaps barefoot into the flames. His friends join him and clutching their cans of beer, dance around on the red-hot embers.

'How do you do that without getting burnt?' I ask one of them.

'The goddess protects us,' he says.

The zoo

Nat is with his father for the weekend and, feeling bored, I go to the zoo. It's early, and with few visitors around I find myself standing alone in front of the gorilla enclosure. A baby snuggles against its mother's fur, a half-grown youngster is playing with a stick, and their father eyes me from a distance. Then the huge silverback rises and lumbers over to where I'm standing.

I edge closer to the window. So does he, until there is little more than its thickness between us and our noses almost touch. Despite the safety glass I cower before his strength, the rippled muscles of his shoulder, the overhang of his brow.

Instinct tells me to back away but I'm held by the power of his steadfast gaze. Within his eyes I discern a wisdom at once ancient and unfathomable, and as he continues to stare, I feel him reach deep into my soul. Then he's seen enough, dismisses me, and returns to his family.

I step away from the enclosure wondering what it was he read in my eyes, suspecting that he saw blundering ignorance. Shaken, I walk along a path that meanders through dense vegetation, then emerges into the open alongside a tall wooden fence.

Something blue and muscular drops from above and sweeps across my face like a moist flannel. I look up, and a giraffe throws me a coy glance through curling lashes.

Judith Prosperity

'Not if you're still at sea,' I say, when he asks me to marry him. 'I've been lonely for long enough.' Each time he goes away it's for five long months, and I'm not going to move to Australia to live without him.

As a marine engineer Nick's led an interesting life. He's carried fuel to isolated settlements on the steaming Congo River, been shot at while delivering diesel to Vietnam during the war, and sailed into Rio, where Christ the Redeemer reaches out his arms from Corcovado Mountain.

He tells me that when he was first at sea, oil tankers tied up alongside the refineries and took days to disgorge their cargo, allowing their crews to explore the port and its surrounds. The Japanese tankers on which he sails these days reload within hours at off-shore terminals.

Mostly now, he sees the sea. Nick needs no persuasion from me. He's ready to come ashore.

But before we can be together he must go away one last time, and I am bound by my teaching contract to remain in Singapore until the end of another school term.

His letters arrive at irregular intervals – wads of white tissue in brown envelopes. I can tell from the dates that he writes every day, but he sends them to me in lots of six or eight when a visiting shipping agent can take them ashore. I read and re-read the neatly formed lines written in a semi-darkened cabin after a twelve-till-four watch, and I learn things about my future husband that spoken words would not have told.

He's been gone for three months when I arrive home from school one afternoon, my arms weighed down by classwork. The children have been studying grasses, and I have twenty-four squares of green canvas on which they've embroidered the leafy stems. The flowing stitches are pleasing, but to do the pictures justice, I need to mount them.

I'm sitting on my pink-tiled floor, sticky-fingered and surrounded by bits of card, when the phone rings. A woman gives the name of a shipping agent and tells me to be on a certain jetty at midnight. Then she rings off.

It can mean only one thing. Nick's ship is sailing into Singapore.

At eleven thirty, apprehensive and exhilarated, I drive my Spitfire down a still brilliantly lit Orchard Road. Soon after, I leave the shopping centres behind and turn into deserted streets lined with shuttered factories and warehouses.

When I reach the jetty it's in darkness, but I can hear water lapping against the wall. I get out of the car and walk along the road until I find a small launch in which three men are working.

One of them calls out to me. 'Sally?'

When I answer, he tells me he's going out to the *Judith Prosperity* and has been instructed to take me with him. He holds out his hand and helps me down into the boat, where an old Chinese man is fiddling with the motor. I smile uncertainly and say hello. He looks at me and then solemnly bows his head.

With a burst of smoke the engine comes to life.

What am I doing in a boat in the middle of the night, heading into the vastness of Singapore harbour with three strangers?

Before I can have second thoughts, we putter away from the wharf in water stinking of diesel and rotten fish. We speed away and, leaving behind a frothy white trail, head for the open sea. For almost an hour no one speaks. The twinkling lights of Singapore city gradually fade away as we draw nearer to the Western Anchorage. The engine slows and the launch edges towards an oil tanker. One of the crew swings a spotlight upward to illuminate the name emblazoned on the ship's bow.

It's not the *Judith Prosperity*. The engine strikes up again and we glide through the outer reaches of the harbour, slipping quietly between sleeping ships, grey elephants in the gloom. The young man points his spotlight onto one hull after another and then, disappointed, swings it away. Time passes, and after so long a silence, the men begin speaking to each other in curt monosyllables and I sense a growing tension between the agent and his crew.

When at last the spotlight picks out the words '*Judith Prosperity*' there are smiles all round. The pictures I've seen must have been of fully laden oil tankers lying low in the water. They haven't prepared me for the reality of the ship's cliff-like sides. I look up to the distant deck where I can make out tiny figures. One, in a white boilersuit, waves. It must be Nick. Now all I need to do is climb this mountain.

A platform hangs at sea level below a steel gangway. The agent grips my arm and as the launch rises with the swell, urges me to jump.

Displaying a confidence I don't feel, I leap across the void and begin the long climb to the deck. Then I'm at the top and in Nick's arms.

We can't stop giggling. It's all so delightfully unexpected, this reunion at sea. His cabin is more spacious than I had envisaged. He sleeps in a double bed, there's an armchair, a desk and even a hanging plant. Nick closes the door. We fall into each other's arms and for a few precious hours, forget the outside world.

Shortly before daybreak our euphoria is interrupted by a tinny voice on the loud speaker announcing that the shipping agent will be going ashore in fifteen minutes. If I don't want to sail out through the Singapore Roads we will have to say goodbye right away.

I shed no tears and feel only joy at having been given this bonus, this unexpected time together. I clatter down the gangway and although the sea is rougher than when I arrived, easily accomplish the leap back onto the launch. Shortly after, we tie up at the jetty in a pale dawn. I thank the agent and say goodbye.

There isn't enough time to go home so I drive straight to the school. As I arrive children are being dropped off and mothers are chatting together in the car park. In the classroom my Grade Twos are putting away their lunch boxes, and I drop my handbag into my desk drawer.

I'm struck by the normality of it all. It's as if my nighttime foray into the outer reaches of the harbour was in an entirely different reality.

England

Next term will be my last at Tanglin Preparatory because I'm soon to be married and will be joining Nick in Australia. Before school starts I'm flying back to England to see my mother, as it could be a while before I'll be able to visit again.

After the rich greens of the tropics London seems dirty, dark and dreary. Yet when we arrive in Yorkshire I'm shocked by the transformation that has occurred in my home town. Someone has sandblasted the blackened walls of the post office and law courts, and the ancient cathedral now looks as if it were built yesterday.

Angus, Nat and I stay with my mother over Christmas and although she's getting old, she makes a huge effort to ensure we all have a wonderful time.

It's after the festivities are over that my mother and I sit down together, and she tells me how she came to hear of my father's death.

When his calls stopped she had no way of finding out the reason, and was left to wait and wonder. Then a fortnight later a woman phoned with the news that my father was dead. She said he had told her to make the call, but insisted she delay it until two weeks after he was gone. So by the time my mother found out there'd already been a funeral and a cremation. The caller was my father's other 'wife', who had shared his home throughout all the years my mother had awaited his return.

The story comes as no surprise to me. I've suspected all along that my father had someone else.

My mother goes on to tell me how some time later she travelled to London and met this woman in the gardens of the crematorium. There the two scattered my father's ashes together, and afterwards sat on a bench in the sunshine, talking about the man they had both loved – and shared.

I want to know when it was that my father moved in with this person.

'After he sent us back to Yorkshire,' my mother says. 'When he told me he was looking for another apartment. Instead he went to live with her, and she had his son.'

A son!

'Was he at the crematorium with his mother?' I ask, amazed to discover that I now have a half-brother. But he wasn't there, and my mother hasn't met him.

When I ask whether my father was a bigamist, she says the woman told her there'd been a wedding 'of sorts', and at the time she didn't know he had another family. That is, until my father deliberately left a copy of his marriage certificate lying around for her to find.

As for his calls to my mother, every day for thirty years – my father sent the poor woman out of the room before he picked up the phone.

AUSTRALIA

Immigration

When Nat and I return to Singapore, and later move from there to Australia, Angus remains behind. He's a boarder at an old English 'public' school. Unlike some, this one is coeducational and progressive, and he is receiving an education unaffected by our frequent moves from country to country. He seems happy there but I worry about him being so far away, especially since his father works overseas and doesn't plan to return to England. It would be wonderful if Nick, Nat, Angus and I could all live together in Australia. But before that can happen I need to be granted permanent residence. A lot depends on this interview.

We enter a cubicle-like room where a sober-faced man in his thirties is standing behind a table. After a perfunctory handshake we all sit down. Before he can say anything I take a bag of Lego out of my handbag, give it to Nat and suggest that he plays quietly in one corner.

To my surprise the immigration official ignores me and instead proceeds to question Nick at length. He wants to know in what year he first came to Australia, how long he was at sea and whether he intends to remain here permanently. He takes notes while Nick is speaking, and it's impossible to tell from his tight-lipped expression whether he considers the answers to be satisfactory.

By the time he turns to me, I have a dry throat and palpitations.

'Where did you two meet?' he asks.

'Nick had just come off a ship,' I blurt out. 'He picked me up in a bar in Singapore.'

I see the man's raised eyebrows, but for some reason my brain has disconnected itself from my mouth. 'Ginivy's on Orchard Road,' I go on. 'It's a bit of a dive really.'

The man continues to stare at me, and when I glance over and notice the look on Nick's face I realise what I've done. I should have lied. I should have said we met at the prestigious Tanglin Club, or were introduced by mutual friends. Now I've ruined my chance of ever getting a visa.

The official looks over at Nat, quietly building cars in the corner, and back at me. It's then that I notice a slight puckering under his eyes and a twitch at the corner of his lips. All at once he rolls back in his chair, opens his mouth and bursts into laughter.

When he's recovered a little, he says he's heard enough. He can't tell us officially, but it's likely I'll get my visa. He shakes our hands and shows us out.

The waterbed (Part 1)

We begin our new life together by renting a unit in Manly, overlooking Sydney Harbour. It's convenient since Nick, who is working on the ferries, can roll out of bed in the early hours, cross the road and be on board within minutes.

I've brought only a few rugs, lamps and small items from Singapore, and left behind the grand piano that might not have survived the move to a different, drier climate. We've taken a furnished flat, so it's not until Nick is offered a job inspecting oil cargoes in South Australia that we begin to think about buying furniture.

Everyone's raving about waterbeds. Magazines show pictures of film stars posing on huge, circular ones swathed in leopard skin. I think it's Hugh Hefner of *Playboy* who says, 'Waterbeds are good for two things – and sleeping is one of them.'

When we go shopping we see them everywhere: hard sided, soft sided, some with fluffy pink headboards, others with built-in sound systems. We settle for one with ruched velvet padding around its edges and foam baffles inside, designed to limit the wave motion.

We don't fill it immediately. First it has to be delivered to our new home in Whyalla, a steel town built amid the saltbush and red earth of the Spencer Gulf.

Nick goes ahead to meet his new employers and organise the house, and I follow a few days later. By the time I arrive he's already unpacked the furniture and filled the waterbed. He returns to work, leaving me to make it up with our new sheets and pillows.

Now as it happens I'm narrow-shouldered and have skinny upper arms. If I fell into a swimming pool without steps I wouldn't be able to pull myself out. I quickly discover that to lift the bladder and tuck in the sheets I'd need the muscles of Arnold Schwarzenegger. But when Nick returns we work as a team and after our eventual success, fall into bed exhausted.

I discover that waterbeds are indeed good for sleeping on as long as you don't mind riding the wave each time your partner turns over. And yes, they're sexy too, if you don't get seasick.

The Rover 12

As Hitler marched into Poland my mother was having her first driving lesson. With war declared, the British government suspended all testing, and a licence was issued without her ever having to prove she was safe on the road.

As it happened, after learning the basic rudiments, she didn't drive a car again for nearly twenty years. For all that time she lugged her shopping home on the bus. There was a green Rover 12 in the garage, but that only emerged at weekends when Grandpa took us to York for a boat trip down the Ouse, or onto Ilkley Moor for a family picnic. Even when, in his eighties, his heart began to fail, Grandpa wouldn't trust my mother with his car.

But then one day he was gone. A week after the funeral my mother discovered the key to the Rover hidden at the back of a little drawer in Grandpa's roll-top desk. It was time to take up motoring again. A few lessons might have been in order but my mother, who had an overwhelming confidence in her driving ability, ignored that suggestion and planned a holiday instead. We'd all have a week at the seaside.

Miraculously, she drove both ways without hitting anything, apart that is, from the stone bollard that for some unaccountable reason rose from the middle of a deserted Welsh beach. I know my mother saw it when it was some distance away, because she commented on it.

'I couldn't decide whether to pass it on the left or the right,' she said afterwards. 'But it's just the bumper. That's easily fixed.'

Once home, I vowed never to get into a car with her again.

Over the following years she used the Rover when she went shopping, visited friends or had an afternoon at the bowling club. I was living overseas, so I only heard of her little 'incidents' when she chose to tell me about them over the telephone.

'That new motorway's confusing,' she said one evening when I was living in Singapore. 'I had an awful shock. A car came straight at me. It wasn't until I nearly hit a truck that I found out I was going the wrong way.'

'What did you do? I asked, horrified. 'Did you pull over?'

'No,' she said. 'It was fine. I drove on for a mile or so until I found somewhere to turn off.'

She lived for a while with a friend in a house situated at the high end of a quiet grove. She told me how she'd arrived home from bowls one afternoon, parked, and had then gone to unfasten the gate. Concerned that on such a windy day it might swing back and damage the car, she pushed it hard against the fence so its bottom bolt was safely wedged into the concrete.

When she turned around her car had gone.

She stared up and down the empty street. It had taken less than a minute to secure the gate. Surely that wasn't long enough for someone to steal a car, even if it was unlocked?

She set off down the hill, checking side roads and driveways as she went. At a point where the grove swung around a sharp bend before joining the highway she found her car. It was sitting on the nature strip with its nose hard up against a mountain ash. There was a bit of damage she told me, but it was soon fixed.

As she grew older, my mother's eyes became clouded by cataracts. I suggested that for safety reasons it would be better to give up her car; that an occasional taxi would cost less than its running costs. Besides, a bus ran past the end of her street every fifteen minutes. She could use that. My mother didn't agree.

'What about an operation?' I asked, having heard that cataracts could be successfully treated.

'The doctor says I have to wait until my eyes get really bad before he does them.'

'But isn't it dangerous to go on driving?'

'It's not a problem. I can't see in sunlight, but I'm fine as long as I stick to roads I know well and only drive in dull daylight.'

'But what if the sun comes out while you're in the car?'

She didn't answer.

Not long after, my mother embarked on the long flight to Australia and came to stay with us in Whyalla.

'Let's do a little test,' suggested my husband when we were returning from shopping one evening. 'There's a sign up ahead. Tell me when you can read it.'

'Give Way,' cried my mother triumphantly – when Nick was already turning onto the highway.

The waterbed (Part 2)

We enjoy living in Whyalla despite its isolation, but Nick isn't entirely happy in his job. A year later, when a position becomes available in Victoria, we decide to move on. A suitable rental property is hard to find but we settle for an old weatherboard in Castlemaine. It has four rooms off a central hallway, a kitchen tacked onto the back and a toilet across the yard.

Our first job after moving in is to fill the bed. It takes forty-eight hours to warm up, and as we don't want to die of hypothermia during the night, we sleep on the floor. When we *are* able to lie in it again, we discover that during the emptying and refilling something nasty has happened to the baffles. When Nick turns over now, I'm aboard a ship in a storm and at risk of being swept overboard.

Our dog falls asleep one afternoon in the bedroom doorway with her ball between her paws. Of its own accord it rolls off across the floor in the direction of the waterbed. It's then that I remember reading about another couple who rented an old house like ours. As they filled their waterbed, the bedroom, which had been an add-on, slowly parted company with the rest of the house. The thought of it makes me nervous.

Sheep

Angus completes his schooling in Castlemaine and while he waits to go off to university, works for a builder renovating an abbatoir.

I'm in the middle of washing up one morning when he calls to tell me he's found a newborn lamb. It's wandering around the holding yards, crying for a mother that has already been slaughtered. If it's not fed soon it'll die. Will I take it?

I've cared for a lamb before, but only for a night. I know a lot about dogs. Nothing about sheep. But how can I refuse?

I pick up an old blanket and drive to where Angus has told me to stand ready under the abattoir wall. He calls out a warning and then drops a sack over for me to catch. When I peer inside I see a tiny, pathetic creature covered in mud. Gently, I lay it on my knee and drive home.

Within hours it's dead, and I feel terrible.

Afterwards I contact a man I've been told knows all about sheep. 'It probably didn't have a first feed from its mother,' he says. 'It wouldn't have stood a chance without the antibodies in her milk.'

I'm just getting over the trauma when a week later, the phone rings again. It's Angus with another sheep. Can I come and get it?

I'm better equipped this time. I have a suitable bottle and teat and a tin of dried milk designed for orphaned farm animals.

This lamb is bigger than the one that died and seems generally stronger. The weather's too cold for little Peter to stay outside at night and he has to be fed every few hours. There's only one place for him – in the bathroom. I make a bed of straw under the basin.

The following morning I'm washing my face and talking to Peter at the same time, when the phone rings. It's Angus. Another lamb is frantically searching for its mother. Can I come and get it?

I ask him how much longer he'll be working at the abattoir.

He says this is his last week. I leave Peter asleep in the bathroom and go to rescue another lost soul. This one is female. I feed her sitting on my lap, decide to call her Pe-on-y and ensure I'm wearing a waterproof apron next time. Stockier than Peter, Peony is confident and demanding – a very different creature. Anyone who believes farm animals don't have personalities is deluding himself.

During the day the lambs follow me around the house and at night Peony joins Peter in the bathroom. When they are stronger I let them outside to play, but there's a problem. We don't have a proper garden, just a concrete path that runs around the house, edged by a few shrubs. There's one small tree and a goldfish pond.

Minutes after Peter goes outside he falls into it. Luckily I'm in the garden too and am able to pull him out in time. I carry him into the bathroom and switch on my hairdryer. His wool is pure white, thick and fluffy.

From then on I tether the pair to the clothes line if I'm not going to be around. They don't seem to mind. Of course the children love them, and it's not long before Nat has taught Peter to butt a tennis ball. Peony refuses to play, but then she's willful and not as smart as her brother.

When they grow too big for the bathroom we clear out our little garden shed and they sleep in there at night. I have to rise at dawn because the moment they're awake they make a terrible row and I don't want any trouble from our neighbours.

I'm weaning them slowly. We don't have a lawn, so I pick grass from the side of the road and chop it up for them. One afternoon I see them nibbling the weeds that grow between the cracks in the concrete path.

The next day I let them into the garden as usual, but when I check on them later I can see that something is wrong. Their ears and noses have turned bright red and the skin is peeling off. It looks like sunburn – but it can't be. It's not even summer and besides, whoever heard of a sheep that couldn't cope with a bit of sunshine?

It's a struggle, but somehow I manage to squeeze them both into my car and drive them around to the vet's. And yes, it *is* sunburn. Apparently the little weeds they ate are poisonous and they've caused a photo-allergic reaction. From now on I will have to rub zinc cream onto the lambs' ears and noses every morning before I let them out – but only for six weeks or so.

As Peter and Peony grow bigger, so does their demand for food. We take to the 'long paddock' and I spend a lot of time sitting on grass verges watching them eat. I know I can't keep them much longer, but I fear for them. After all my loving care I don't want them turned into chops.

Then a friend who has two acres of lawn around his house mentions he's sick of mowing and would like some sheep to keep the grass down. He doesn't have a fence, so he needs to find some that are easy to handle and willing to be tethered.

And I just happen to know where there's a couple like that.

Late

The car won't start. I know what it is, of course. My husband's been telling me for days to buy a new battery. This has to happen when I'm off to a job interview. I can't get a jump start because Nick's not home.

I look at my watch and race inside to call a taxi. Then I run to the car to grab my documents and certificates off the front seat, race back into the house again because I've left my handbag by the phone, have a quick glance in the mirror and lock up. Already breathless, I run out to the road.

I need this job. I haven't found a school willing to employ me, I've had no luck applying for other work, and I've learnt that teaching skills aren't taken into account when you're trying out for lollipop lady. A position as an instructor in a centre for the intellectually disabled, however, could herald the beginning of a whole new career. But if the taxi doesn't arrive in the next five minutes I can forget about that.

At last I see it coming and wave to the driver. He pulls over and I jump in, knowing I'm going to be late, but not very late. As we set off I tell him I'm in a desperate hurry to get to an interview and he's sympathetic to the point of almost running a red light.

He drops me off in front of the centre, a low redbrick building with a small fenced garden out the front. I pay him and hurry to the door, passing several physically and obviously intellectually disabled people on the way. They smile at me and come up to say hello, and right away I know that if I do get the job I'll enjoy working with them.

As I step inside the front door I look again at my watch and with a sudden dryness in my throat, realise that I should have arrived ten minutes ago. Waiting outside the director's office is a tall distinguished man with looks vaguely reminiscent of Errol Flynn. I introduce myself, tell him I've come for the interview, and say I'm sorry I'm late. When I begin to explain how my car broke down, he shrugs off my apologies and warmly shakes my hand.

'Would you like to have a look around first?' he asks.

'Thank you,' I say, 'I'd like that.'

He leads me down a narrow corridor decorated with the participants' artwork and shows me into an airy hall where half a dozen young men are drinking tea and passing around a plate of jam scones.

'You'll have to do lunch duty if you work here,' my hopefully-boss-to-be says. 'It means giving out the medication.'

'That won't be a problem.'

He takes me into the kitchen where elderly ladies are rolling out pastry, and afterwards shows me an area set aside for indoor sport. Then he invites me to look through the window of the craft room, where an instructor is showing a woman in a wheelchair how to hook wool into a rug. Finally, when I'm beginning to wonder how much longer it will be before we commence the formal part of the interview, the director leads me back to his office.

At the door he leans forward and whispers in my ear, 'How do you like my moustache?'

I jerk back as if I've been stung.

At that instant a bearded man in a tweed jacket emerges from the office.

'You're supposed to be in the workshop. Go and join your group,' he tells my companion.

Then turning to me, he says, 'You here for the interview? You're very late.'

The waterbed (Part 3)

Within a couple of years we're on the move again – this time to Bendigo. As usual our first task after taking over a new house is to heave the bladder into its position on the wooden frame. Nick attaches a hose to the tap in the garden, and since it's a slow process, leaves the bed to fill while he goes off to do another job. I clean up the kitchen, then decide it's time to do some washing. On my way to collect the soiled clothes I notice the hall carpet is wet and water is seeping under the bedroom door.

When I open it I'm confronted by a whale. A fountain of water is spurting out of its blowhole and cascading over the sides of the bed. 'Nick!' I scream.

He comes running into the room.

'Quick,' he says. 'Race outside and turn off the tap.'

But I can't because I'm down on my knees, doubled up with laughter.

The carpets have to be taken up and thrown out. They're not only soaked but now have that familiar, rotting-algae smell peculiar to waterbeds.

Not long afterwards we decide that our bed will have to go. It's when we wake one night to wet sheets and discover that we've sprung a leak. Of course I'm the one responsible – never leave bobby pins in your hair if you sleep on a waterbed.

A burglary

Sometime after moving to Bendigo to be nearer to work, we buy a house surrounded by ten acres of bush and farmland. It's eleven o'clock in the morning and I'm at work when my husband calls. 'Can you come home right away? We've been burgled.'

As I turn into the driveway I see a police car parked in front of the house. When I go inside I find a uniformed officer standing on a chair in the laundry with his head in the access hole to the roof cavity. In a moment he jumps down.

'It's okay,' he says. 'I've checked. There's no one up there.'

Nick is in the kitchen. 'I forgot some papers,' he tells me. 'I came back to collect them and saw the sliding door wide open, so I knew someone had broken in. I called the police. Then it struck me that the burglars might still be in the house, so I ran back outside.'

'What's missing?'

'I don't know yet. I haven't had time to check.'

I follow him into the living room. The television is in its usual place. Were the burglars disturbed before they had time to take anything? One glance into our bedroom instantly dispels that thought. The drawers of the bedside tables have been wrenched out and thrown onto the floor and worse, much worse, my underwear is spread out across the bed.

Overcome by a wave of nausea, I sink into a chair. But when I hear the policeman's footsteps in the corridor my discomfort suddenly gives way to embarrassment. Scooping up three pairs of knickers with flagging elastic more grey than white, I hastily kick them under the bed and out of sight. Then claustrophobic and sick, I rush past the officer and into the kitchen.

I'm standing in front of the sink filling a glass with water when it hits me. They've taken my jewellery. I hurry back into the bedroom and scrabble through the piles of clothing dumped on the bed and the floor. Yes, it's all gone.

When I describe my missing bracelets and necklaces to the policeman he gives me a look and says he's calling in senior detectives. What he thought was a common break-in has suddenly escalated into a major jewellery heist.

Within minutes a second officer arrives and begins checking the windows for signs of entry. My thoughts turn immediately to the sliding glass door in the kitchen, where I soon discover scratches in the brown paint around the lock.

'This is where they got in,' I call out to the officer. 'You can see the marks where they used a tool to force open the door.'

He wanders over and gives the paint a cursory glance. 'No,' he says, 'they're not recent. They left those marks the last time they were here.'

I stare at him.

'Didn't you know this place has been broken into before? We've been here twice in the last few weeks.'

'I'd no idea. We've only recently moved in.'

What have we done? We chose this house because it was well away from the road and the surrounding bush offered peace and tranquillity. It didn't occur to me that it might provide cover for thieves.

Before they leave one of the officers recommends that we put locks on all the windows. We will, but it seems pointless. Our nearest neighbour lives way across the paddock and you could smash our windows with a sledgehammer without him hearing.

The policeman offers other advice. 'Just in case they came on foot, it might be worth checking the bush around the house. Sometimes, if they're in a hurry, they grab all sorts of things indiscriminately. When they get a safe distance away they dump anything that's too heavy to carry or they think they can't sell.'

It sounds like a waste of time. Nevertheless, when I return home from work that evening I walk into the forest nearest to the house and search among the fallen leaves. I don't find anything.

The next day an assessor from the insurance company arrives. I've prepared a list of missing items, at least the ones we've identified so far. It's an odd mixture: the Malay knife that has gone from the wall in my husband's office, his spare watch, an old camera. They've taken a four-pack of VB beer from the fridge and a bag of pens, Blu-tack and sticky tape that I bought for Nat, who is about to go away to college. They've even taken the five and ten cent coins from his moneybox.

And of course there's my jewellery. I've made detailed drawings of each piece and I hand these to the assessor. He flicks through the pages and then looks around the room. I can tell he's taking stock of the peeling yellow paint, the hideous brown-striped curtains and the awful shag-pile carpet that was full of cat fleas when we moved in.

When I catch his eye he looks away, but I can tell he is studying me too. He's caught me at a bad moment. He arrived as I was digging holes in the front garden for the plants I brought with me from the other house, and I haven't had time to wash. I'm wearing tattered jeans and a baggy old T-shirt I bought in an op shop years ago.

He gets up to leave, but at the door he stops. 'I'd like to remind you,' he says severely, 'that there are heavy penalties for giving a false declaration to an insurance company.'

I feel the blush rise in my cheeks and before I know it, I'm blabbering on about having been given the jewellery by an Arabian sheik. I can tell from the way he looks at me that he doesn't believe a word of it.

My initial enthusiasm for the place has evaporated. In the evenings I drive home from work with a bad feeling in my stomach that worsens when I turn into the driveway. As I get out of the car I scan the yard, searching for anything out of place. I go around to the back of the house and slip my key into the lock, but my other hand automatically reaches for the knob to check whether the door is already undone.

Before I leave for work each day I take our German shorthaired pointer for a walk. Soon after the insurance assessor's visit the weather turns warm, and we follow a path that I've recently discovered, leading to a big dam in the bush.

Coby leaps straight in, her paddling creating ever widening ripples, golden in the early morning light. I turn my face into the sun and

take a few deep, calming breaths. The dog emerges from the water and shakes herself, wetting me in the process, and then runs off along the dam's earth wall. Then she stops to sniff at some alien, man-made object lying in the bushes.

It's my old grey coat! My gardening gloves are lying beside it. The following morning I spot four empty VB bottles under a gum tree.

A few days later I find our old suitcase lying in a gully, wheels in the air. I assume it's empty, but when I look inside I discover a brooch with its pin caught in the lining. A little silver heart crossed by an arrow, it's a sentimental Victorian piece, of no real value. But I'm fond of it and I walk home feeling happier than I have for a while.

Two weeks pass and we hear nothing more from the police or the insurance assessor. Then one morning I wake to find fog blanketing the garden. I get dressed, call out to Coby, and as usual we walk through the bush up to the big dam. A grey mist is rising from its surface and the surrounding gum trees throw lacy patterns onto the water.

Coby circles a tree stump, sniffing. Our neighbour's dogs have probably left their calling cards on the weathered bark. I go over and am about to pull her away when something on the ground sparkles and catches my attention. It's a gold hoop – one of my earrings!

'Come on, Coby,' I say, and together we run back to the house, where my husband is getting dressed.

I tell him what I've found. 'Can you come and help me search the bush? There might be something else.'

He puts on his shoes and we go up the path together. At the dam we separate and walk around it in opposite directions, carefully examining the stony ground. Fifteen minutes pass without either of us finding anything. Soon we'll have to give up the search and go to work.

Nick calls out. 'Any luck?'

'No.' But as I look out across the water, I see something glitter.

'Look! Behind you!'

The sun, breaking through the mist, has set alight a shining garland adorning a little, out-of-season Christmas tree. I run over to Nick, who is staring at it in amazement, and together we strip my necklaces and bracelets from the branches. Once we've rescued everything hanging in the tree, we crouch down in the damp earth at its roots and find another pendant and my pearl earrings. Now only a few items are missing, and we return home to call the police and the insurance agent and tell them the good news.

In the evening the assessor returns. I see his expression change as he picks up a heavy gold bracelet and runs it through his fingers. Suddenly he's eager to compensate us for the old camera, the Malay knife and the watch that kept stopping. And he makes it clear that he doesn't intend to argue over their value.

Living in the bush as I do, I've little use for fancy jewellery, and over the years I've gradually sold or given it away, which is a pity, because now I've nothing to show anyone to whom I've told this story. As a result, when I've finished telling it I usually receive the same doubting looks that I had from the insurance assessor.

Country music festival

Nick parks the car in a roped-off area of the grassy oval and we walk toward the stage. This is our first festival and although neither of us is a big fan of country music, we're looking forward to a relaxing day outdoors, picnicking and listening to live performances.

We're early. Stallholders are arranging cowboy hats, CDs and lucky-dip bags on umbrella-shaded tables. We cross to the rows of plastic chairs, assailed by booms and squeaks emanating from where two

youths are working on the sound equipment. Locals lift blue-and-white coolers from the boots of old Fords. There's laughter and calling out as friends and relatives find each other and organise their seating.

A huge man in a cowboy hat looks up at the cloudless blue sky and remarks, 'It's going to be a hot'n.'

Mothers rub sunscreen onto wriggling children and then shout, 'Put on your hat!' as they break free and run off to look at the souvenir stall.

The efforts of the first band are largely ignored as men crack open footie results with their mates. The musicians generate a half-hearted, ragged handclap at the end of each number. Three bands follow one another in quick succession. A DJ from the local radio station introduces them in turn, vainly attempting to arouse interest with a few lame jokes.

It's getting warm. I buy a bottle of lemonade and take off my cardigan. More cars arrive and the chairs begin to fill. As the next set comes to an end, a white bus pulls into the parking area and a dozen young men climb out. They stand around it, waiting until the last of them is lifted down and helped into his wheelchair. Then their carer leads the way across the grass toward us.

Some of the men could take their places among the audience without being given a second glance, but others are visibly different. A cheerful young man with straw-blond hair has the give-away features of Down syndrome. Another is unusually tall, and when a high-pitched, bird-like cry bursts from his lips, he immediately catches the attention of the crowd.

A woman with underarm hair and a pink tank top stretched over a protruding navel, nudges her husband. 'Look, it's the retards from the Boys' Home.'

The men file down the centre aisle and settle into seats in the front row. When the band begins the next number they are up on their feet in an instant, waving gawky arms in the air as they dip and swing to the music. The man in the wheelchair laughs out loud and beats out the rhythm on his knees.

One of his friends grabs his chair and whirls it around and he whoops in delight. The musicians onstage increase their efforts, encouraged by the dancers' natural exuberance. But around me I hear whispering.

'They shouldn't be encouraged to make an exhibition of themselves,' mutters a narrow-faced woman to my left.

A man sitting immediately behind her agrees. 'It's their carer's fault. He should have seated them at the back where they wouldn't have bothered anybody.'

A musician in a black cowboy shirt and ragged jeans limps onto the stage and tunes his guitar. He doesn't look like much, but as soon as he starts to play it's obvious to everyone that there is sweet music in the man. Friends stop their chatter and froth overflows from beer cans as they are tapped against knees in time with the beat.

A young girl jumps up and pulls at her boyfriend's arm. 'Come on, Kev, dance with me.'

But he hasn't drunk enough for that. 'Aw, Cathy, if you want to dance do it by yourself. No one's stopping you.'

She sits down again, sulking.

By twelve thirty the sausage sizzle is doing brisk business and a queue forms. Two men in green aprons fold the meat into slices of flabby white bread while ketchup seeps through like blood on a bandage. Women slice up half-frozen cheesecakes, kids bite into pink-iced doughnuts covered in sprinkles, and empty beer cans are crushed underfoot as the first bottles of wine appear.

The men from the Boys' Home eat their sandwiches. At a signal from their carer they stand up and walk over to the drinks stall to buy cans of Coke.

By mid-afternoon the beer and wine have done their work and the grass in front of the stage is filled with dancing revellers. Some who have been drinking steadily since early morning, stagger around spilling beer from their stubbies and bumping into each other. But nobody seems to care – after all, they're just ordinary folk having a good time, aren't they?

The men in the front row stand up and walk back to their bus. They've clearly had a wonderful day, but now it's time to go home.

Coby and the vet

The thin light of dawn is filtering through the curtains when I first hear her soft, padding footsteps outside our bedroom door. Coby, our shorthaired pointer, has always been a sound sleeper, so I know something is amiss. I get up and peer out into the darkened hallway.

She's pacing – back and forth, up and down, between bedroom and kitchen. There's something automatic about the way she moves that makes me wonder whether she's sleepwalking. Or does she need to go outside to relieve herself?

She follows me to the back door but when I open it she stops, looks outside, seems momentarily confused, and then returns to her pacing. I take hold of her collar and persuade her to follow me into the bedroom where, after a few minutes, she lies down and goes back to sleep.

In the morning I puzzle over her behaviour, unsure of its significance. Coby's an old dog. She's fifteen. She's deaf too, and the brown-mottled pelt that once shone like satin in the sun now hangs slackly over her gaunt frame. At bedtime one cushion is no longer enough. Arthritis has gnawed away at her bones, stiffening her back and preventing her from curling into her favourite sleeping position.

I saw a wet patch on her cushion when she stood up to greet me one morning and I recognised, with sinking heart, that she'd become incontinent. I took her to the vet, an older man I hadn't previously met. Expecting the worst, I told him about that problem, and about her weight loss and arthritis. He listened to her heart and then gave me some pills to stop the wetting.

Rubbing her ears, he said, 'She's a remarkable old dog. Pointers don't usually reach her age, but while she's happy we'll nurse her along and keep her comfortable.'

And now this strange, nighttime pacing. I decide to ignore it. After all, she eats well and still enjoys lengthy walks in the bush.

Then one evening when we're watching television, Coby stands up and begins circling the coffee table. Round and round she goes until, with difficulty, I manage to pull her away and settle her down again on her bed.

The following morning I hear whimpering coming from the kitchen and discover her trapped in a corner, her head swinging from side to side in a vain attempt to escape. Something has occurred inside the brain of our beautiful, highly intelligent companion, robbing her of the ability to turn around or walk backwards. Her distress is obvious.

It isn't long since our neighbour, who had been diagnosed with Alzheimer's, started a fire by boiling an electric kettle on her gas stove. It's heartbreaking to see a life deteriorate into misery and confusion. At least dogs can be spared that.

My husband and I talk it over. Next day I tell a colleague I'm going to phone the vet and arrange for my dog to be euthanised.

'Don't do that!' he cries in alarm. 'I had a dog put down once. As soon as the needle went in he began howling and thrashing around. It was terrible. It went on for several minutes.'

I stare at him, horrified. I imagined 'putting your dog to sleep' meant just that – a gentle loss of consciousness.

'Did you call the vet?' Nick asks that night.

I haven't. I've been too afraid.

In the morning I'm awoken by Coby's anguished cries and I find her trapped in a corner again, this time in the living room. I know I have to make that call.

'I'm sorry,' the vet says, when I tell him what's been happening. 'There's nothing more I can do. It really is her time now.'

'I know you're right,' I say, 'but I'm scared of having her put down.' I describe my workmate's experience.

'Trust me,' the vet says. 'I promise you, she won't suffer at all. I can come out to your house if you like, so she won't be disturbed unnecessarily.'

I thank him and stay home the following day, keeping Coby company.

While we wait I look through our family photographs, where her nose repeatedly pokes out between groups of smiling children.

She's a born hunter, and only months ago that nose swung back and forth in the bush like a mine detector until it picked up a rabbit's scent. Then with whooping cries she was away, mind and body utterly absorbed in the thrill of the chase.

Her headstrong behaviour might well have led to her death. She became impaled on a thorn bush while chasing a rabbit and once, in hot pursuit of a duck, she leapt into the swollen River Murray and was almost swept away.

She considered cats fair game too, and followed a ginger tom right into its own home. We were walking past a nearby house another day when she squeezed under a hedge and reappeared with a big white hen in her mouth. Cowards, we turned and ran.

My mother visited us when we lived in Whyalla, and I asked her if she would mind watering the lawn while I was at work. On my return I noticed only half of it was wet.

'It was the dog,' she told me. 'She was sleeping over by the flowerbeds. I was about to turn the sprinkler in that direction when she gave me such a disgusted look that I couldn't do it.'

I knew what she meant. The offspring of champions, Coby is a true aristocrat.

For the last time, we walk together in the bush. Then I carry her cushions into the spare bedroom and sit with her, stroking her neck. After a while I hear my husband open the door for the vet and in a moment he tiptoes into the room, a syringe ready in his hand. Startled, Coby lifts her head and her ears shoot back, but the man whispers something to her and she calms again.

I feel her body jolt as the green fluid enters her veins. She yawns, rises, and then curls her body into that favourite sleeping position her arthritis has so long denied. She doesn't cry, she doesn't whimper, she doesn't writhe. She's just an old dog setting off in search of new hunting grounds.

The vet sits with me on the floor while we wait for her to drift away. I sense an intimacy with this sweet, kind man that I can't explain. Afterwards I know that something special and unspoken has passed between us.

I look up at him. 'Thank you,' I say, with a lump in my throat. 'I wish we could go so easily when it's our time. And you were right, there was nothing to fear.'

Of course I miss her and always will, but sometimes when I'm walking alone in the bush I feel her spirit close by, and hear again her whoops of joy as she flies between the trees chasing her rabbits.

The sewing room

The doorbell rings. Someone's in the shop. I step out of my office and seeing that everyone else is busy, I go over to serve. Two women are looking at aprons. The elder of the two, a grey-haired lady in a long green cardigan, tries one on.

'My mother's over from the UK and she's looking for a gift to take home,' her daughter tells me. She picks up a calico bag on which a typical Aussie miner's cottage has been printed. 'I'll take this,' she says.

I carry it over to the counter and she watches me wrap it up.

'There's no sign saying it, but I thought these things were made by the intellectually disabled,' she says.

'They are, but we don't advertise it. We want our customers to buy the goods solely because they're beautiful.'

'I admire you for working with those people,' her mother says. 'You must have the patience of a saint.'

I don't respond. It would take too long to tell her how much I love my job. Where else in the world would my workmates call out, 'I love you, Sally!' when I arrive in the morning? Or notice when I'm tired or stressed and come over to give me a hug?

And it's not that I fuss over them or treat them like children. I'm a demanding boss. For too long they've heard insincerity – '*That's a lovely picture, dear*' – when they know perfectly well it's a scribble. If their job is to trim the bags after they've been sewn I want the threads cut to exactly the right length; short enough to be unnoticeable but not so close that a stitch unravels.

'Do you sew these aprons on the premises?' asks the older lady, and when I nod, asks if she and her daughter could see how they are made.

I take them into the workroom behind the shop. Sixteen intellectually disabled workers of varying age and ability are cutting, sewing and trimming canvas satchels, ordered by the Department of Foreign Affairs for a conference in India. The big table in the centre of the room is weighed down with completed orders ready to be packed: 1000 ham bags for David Jones, tutu bags specially designed for a ballet company in Queensland, twenty aprons for the Governor's residence and 100 bags with elephants printed on them for Melbourne Zoo.

Our visitors stop beside two young men who, by working together, have learnt to mark the spots where the handles are to be sewn onto shopping bags. A dark-haired girl who has limited vocabulary but is a gifted artist, is collecting up the spare pins. They have coloured heads, and in front of her are two pincushions into which she has arranged them in delightfully intricate patterns.

The lady in the green cardigan says, 'It's been most interesting. It's good they have something to keep them occupied.'

A group of workers standing nearby, trimming calico bags, hear what she says and exchange glances.

I know what they are thinking.

I'm not 'occupied'. I'm working and earning a wage.

On their way to the door our visitors say hello to Anna, a young woman with Down syndrome who is sitting in front of an industrial overlocker. She shows them how her machine has been specially adapted to make sewing easier.

'It's nice to see there are at least a few things they can do,' the mother says.

Then a cotton breaks. Anna opens a drawer, takes out a pair of tweezers and begins to rethread the machine. There are four separate strands and each must follow its own special path. Some run through tiny, hidden holes, others must be lifted over hooks and threaded in and out of tunnels.

As Anna expertly completes her task, I see our visitors exchange looks.

I know what they are thinking.

I couldn't do that.

Breasts

As I step into the corridor I'm greeted by clapping and a rousing cheer from the nurses, who must also have heard the result of my biopsy. My lymph nodes are clear. I don't require chemotherapy or radiation and I'm going to live after all.

So far I haven't seen the wound, but now a nurse leads me into a private room where she begins unwinding the bandages that swathe my upper body. When she's almost done she asks me to sit down on the bed. I know why. I've heard of women who fainted when they first saw themselves after the operation. The last piece of dressing comes off.

'Ready?' the nurse asks, and when I nod, swings open a wardrobe door revealing a full-length mirror.

I let out a sigh of relief. Having expected an ugly hollow, I see instead a smooth plane and a neat scar, which runs across my chest and disappears under my arm.

The nurse throws me a nervous glance.

'I'm fine,' I reassure her, and she bandages me up again.

Next day I'm visited by a pleasant, soft-spoken woman who, though not in uniform, tells me she too is a nurse. She sits down beside my bed and asks after my health.

'You'll be going home in a few days,' she tells me, 'and you'll need something to fill up that space in your bra.' She opens her bag and pulls out a pink-striped gift box; the sort that sometimes holds bars of soap or tubes of hand cream.

She removes the lid. I lean forward to look inside – and jerk back as if I've touched a live wire. A piece of flesh is lying in the box. My flesh. The breast they cut from my body. Overtaken by a swirl of nausea I fall dizzily back onto the pillows.

The nurse, clearly horrified by my reaction, claps the lid back on the box and apologises for upsetting me.

'It's only silicone,' she says, 'but I have known other women who thought it was a raw chicken fillet.'

I don't tell her what *I* thought it was.

She waits until I'm feeling better and then puts the box on the bedside cabinet. 'You don't have to look at it now,' she says, 'but please take it with you when you go home. Believe me, you'll want to use it later on.'

I don't think so. My appearance doesn't matter. I'm more concerned about the possibility of the cancer spreading or the wound not healing. Nevertheless, before I leave hospital the box is put into the bag along with my other belongings and, once home, I hide it in the back of the wardrobe where it remains unopened all winter.

Then spring comes, and one pleasant Sunday morning my husband suggests a drive and perhaps lunch in nearby Castlemaine. After browsing for a while in a bookshop we cross the road to a café where tables are set out on the pavement. We order toasted sandwiches. It's the first time since my operation that it's been warm enough to sit outdoors. I shrug off my winter coat, hang it on the back of a chair and relax in the sunshine.

'Shall we have coffee now?' I ask when we've finished eating. 'Double-shot long black?'

Nick nods. Inside, the café is crowded and noisy. As I walk towards the counter a man seated at a table near the window glances casually in my direction. And that's when I remember I'm not wearing my coat. Everyone can see I have one breast. Mortified, I hold my right arm in front of my chest and blunder between the tightly packed tables to escape back outside.

'What's wrong?' asks Nick, watching me grab my coat, pull it on and button it up. When we're in the car, I tell him.

As soon as we arrive home, I go to the wardrobe and take down the pink box with the all-too-realistic breast. Gingerly lifting the lid I discover that I can now look at it calmly, but a shiver of revulsion runs down my back when I try to touch its clammy surface. Fortunately the manufacturers have supplied a cover, and once Nick has stretched that over the offending object, it loses its power over me.

Next day I go to Myer to be measured for a mastectomy bra. The shop assistant is discreet and kind, but the bra's broad straps and heavy pink material indicate that it has come straight from a surgical supplier. Never again will I wear those sexy, lacy little bras from Target. I take it home and weep.

When I show the contraption to Nick, he pulls a face. 'Why don't you put that pad inside your normal bra?' he asks.

I can't. I've searched the net and read the stories of other mastectomy patients. Women all around the world are dropping breasts into their soup, thrashing across swimming pools in pursuit of escapees from the tops of bathers, or chasing dogs who refuse to relinquish their new toys. At least my mastectomy bra has a pocket in which the prosthesis can be safely secured.

'You could sew press studs onto the cover and fasten it inside your usual bra,' suggests Nick.

I try it and it's an immediate success. I describe the process on the net and soon women as far apart as Canada and India are following my example and throwing away their ugly mastectomy bras.

Two years pass and I gradually become less afraid of the cancer returning and more dissatisfied with the shape of my body. It's not that I was ever proud of my breasts. I've always envied those who had something more worthwhile than my meagre mounds to fill out their blouses. Fully clothed I feel like other women, but when I'm naked I find my body's lack of symmetry humiliating. When I can bear it no longer, I visit a plastic surgeon to discuss a possible reconstruction.

I'm stunned when he asks, 'How big would you like your breasts?'

I never expected anything good to come from a diagnosis of cancer, but now amazingly, well into my fifties, I am to have the breasts I could only have dreamed of when I was a teenager.

Gas tanks

My husband's company is responsible for the safety of gas tanks all over Australia. When he first invited me to join him on one of his inspection runs I was unenthusiastic, anticipating lengthy journeys broken by calls at factories and farms where I would wait, bored, until he'd finished his work. But to my delight I found that our trips gave me the opportunity to visit all manner of interesting and unlikely places.

I met factory workers, winemakers and orchardists, lonely chicken farmers desperate for a chat, and funeral directors who needed gas for their cremations. All were friendly and often generous.

'Do you like mangoes?' one Queenslander asked me as Nick was completing an inspection of his tank.

'Yes, thank you. A couple would be nice.'

The man disappeared into his shed and returned instead with a bottle of mango wine. At another property, farm workers were loading fruit onto a truck.

'How about a watermelon?'

And for the next 600 kilometres the green balls rolled around in the back of our hire car. How can two people get through five warm watermelons in less than a week? I thought then of the inspector who drove around with another gift, four trays of eggs, strapped into his front seat for a fortnight.

Before arriving at each property Nick attempted to contact the owner by phone. If he was unsuccessful and no one came to the door, he walked around to the back, found the tank and was away again within minutes. That wasn't without risk.

Once, Nat, who also works in the business, arrived at a property that appeared deserted. He could see the gas tank from where he was standing by the gate, but on the other side were two Great Danes. Who knew what those giants might do to an uninvited stranger?

He went off to complete other scheduled inspections in the area and when he returned the dogs had gone. Relieved, he opened the gate and walked up the long driveway. He was almost at his destination when two fearsome heads appeared from around the side of the tank, under which the dogs had been sleeping. Luckily they were friendly.

Sometimes when I travelled with Nick the tanks were hard to find, and even asking for directions in the local post office wasn't always enough. But the postmistress would soon find someone who, while waving an arm, would say, 'It's eighty kilometres up a bumpy dirt road – roughly in that direction.'

If he was stuck Nick phoned the tanker driver who delivered the gas.

'Do you know where it is?' I once heard him say. 'It's the one where a frog lives under the dome.'

And the driver knew it well.

I learnt that all manner of animals live around gas tanks: cats, goats and lonely horses. Flocks of sheep took off across the paddock as we approached, sometimes leaving just one, hand reared and eager for a pat.

On one occasion Nick, struggling to read an inspection tag, leant forward and took off his glasses in order to see it better, only to have them unexpectedly wrenched from his hand by a pet ostrich.

We saw other birds too: brolgas, spoonbills, stone curlew – and in a vineyard in Western Australia, red-tailed black cockatoos feeding on pine cones.

At the end of a long day travelling over rough country roads we settled for the nearest motel, often one with cheap chairs, dingy lighting and a too-firm bed.

But up on the Atherton Tablelands we stayed in a rainforest lodge where sugar gliders parachuted between the trees and red-legged pademelons grazed on the lawn.

In Tasmania we rented a cabin beside a river where platypus played and where, in the evening, the proprietor scattered mutton bones across our verandah. After dark Tasmanian Devils crept out of the forest and set upon them, and twice during the night I was awoken by snapping, growling, and the sound of teeth grinding on bone.

Bushfire

It's Saturday afternoon and we're having a party, twenty of us sitting together on the verandah talking, drinking and enjoying the beauty of the bush. After a while someone takes out a guitar and we start to sing.

Two more friends arrive. They apologise for being late and tell us they've had to make a detour after driving through smoke. Apparently it's quite dense on the other side of town. Everyone's suddenly alert, sniffing the air and looking around.

This is February, and bushfire season. The fire can't be anywhere nearby because there are no flying embers and not a hint of smoke in the air. We decide there's no cause for concern and continue with the party.

Around six there's a repeated *whup whup* sound overhead and we spot a helicopter hovering above the trees. We watch it drop a line down to what must be a dam hidden in the bush. It hovers for a while and then flies off. Two minutes later, it's back. Suddenly I'm nervous. How far away is that fire?

My husband decides to check, and drives up the road. On his return he tells us not to worry because although he's seen smoke, it's not close and the wind's driving the fire away from us. Our guests discuss the situation and decide they're safer staying where they are and there's no point in breaking up the party. I serve dinner. Afterwards we catch up on each other's news and as darkness falls, light the candles and enjoy a relaxing evening together.

We leave the cleaning up for the morning. There are empty cans to be dumped into the bin, chairs to be stacked and tables folded and returned to the garage. Tired, and a little hung over, I decide a walk will do me good. I set off down the drive to retrieve the balloons I hung up to show our friends where we lived. I can see from a distance they are still there, tied to the signpost and bobbing about in the wind.

A car turns into the dirt road, passes me, reverses into our driveway and swings around. Surprisingly, it's followed by another and then another.

I understand why, when I reach the corner. A police car is parked on the bitumen in the middle of the road and an officer is stopping drivers

and making them turn around. I untie the balloons and with them in my hand, walk over to him.

He tells me that several houses in our street have been burned to the ground, the nearest less than a kilometre from where we are standing. I look down at my balloons, embarrassed and ashamed. While we have been partying our neighbours have endured all kinds of horror, and some have lost everything.

I hurry back to the house where my husband has turned on the television. They're calling it Black Saturday; 173 people are dead and over 2000 homes have been destroyed, sixty-one of them a short distance from ours.

Summer will never be the same again. I check the CFA website and listen to the radio. When the wind rises on hot February afternoons I walk outside to sniff the air and search the horizon for smoke. Once, mistaking 'burning off' for a wildfire, I grabbed our dogs and a few favourite possessions, raced to the garage and drove away.

When I understood it was a false alarm I turned around and discovered that of all the things I'd accumulated over the years, those I cared about didn't even fill the back of a car.

Joan of Arc

For fifty years, Joan of Arc sat on the living-room mantelpiece at home, a witness to the family's joys and sorrows, disagreements and reconciliations, and finally to the deaths of my grandparents.

Then the house was sold and my mother, who since childhood had loved Joan's pensive gaze and piously folded hands, took the bronze statue away with her to the small terrace house she rented farther down the road.

The years rolled on until eventually, half-crippled with arthritis, my mother wearied of Yorkshire's sleeting rain and arctic conditions. She celebrated her eightieth birthday – and emigrated.

Aside from her clothes she brought little with her to Australia. Only a few cherished belongings inherited from my grandmother: a Moorcroft biscuit barrel, a mahogany table, the mug given to Great-Uncle Liddell in 1865 when he became Chief Constable of Newark and, of course, Joan of Arc.

My mother was in a wheelchair when we met her at the airport and she told us she didn't expect to live much longer. But to her surprise, the bronchitis and arthritis that had so restricted her way of life in England rapidly dissipated in Victoria's dry warmth.

It wasn't long before she bought a pleasant unit in a retirement village and embarked upon an ambitious round of elderly citizen outings, afternoon teas, church bazaars and indoor bowls competitions. Remarkably for a woman with only one eye, my mother had perfect aim.

She decided to invest what little remained of her money, and knowing that my husband was a shrewd businessman with shares of his own, turned to him for advice. They both enjoyed their weekly discussions on the state of the market.

To manage a busy social life on a small income she needed to budget carefully. Although that was out of necessity it came easily to her, for my grandmother had taught her to spend prudently and waste nothing. In our home, wool from old pullovers was unwound and re-knitted. Brown paper was carefully removed from parcels, ironed, folded and reused. Worn clothes were cut up for rags after their buttons had been unpicked and stored in a jar. Any spare money was saved in my mother's old red moneybox, ready to pay for the piano lessons I so enjoyed but she could ill afford.

My grandmother, who was apprenticed to a dressmaker when she was ten, taught my mother to sew and to make a frock from material most people would consider only enough for a blouse. Ever eager for a bargain, my mother thought nothing of rising at dawn to be first through the door at a sale. Australia's charity shops afforded her a whole new interest in life.

As she aged, I proposed she use some of her money to buy a new bedspread or footstool, or perhaps to have a short holiday. 'You can't take it with you,' I argued, but my mother, determined to leave at least a small legacy behind when she died, shrugged off all my suggestions.

On her ninetieth birthday she announced, 'The last ten years have been my happiest.'

In a new country, and with my father long gone, she had started her life afresh. And although she and I had at times a difficult and confusing relationship, I was glad she had emigrated and lived close by.

Then a few months after her ninety-first birthday she slipped and fell and broke a leg. Because of her failing heart and fibrotic lungs an operation wasn't an option, and two days later she quietly passed away.

I remembered then how she had once shown me a diary in which she'd written detailed instructions for her funeral, and I asked Nick to drive over to the retirement village to retrieve it. Fearful of causing me further distress, he only later revealed what happened.

My mother's room had been exactly as she had left it: china cups on the shelf, photographs of her grandchildren beside her chair, pots of geraniums in the window. Nick searched for the diary in the drawers of my mother's Welsh dresser and then checked the suitcase under her bed. Finally he discovered it hidden behind a row of shoes in the wardrobe.

Slipping the little book into his pocket, he had one last look around the room before crossing to the door. He placed his hand on the knob and was about to twist it when he felt a strange pressure on his shoulders.

'It was then I heard your mother's voice,' Nick said.

'What do you mean, you heard her voice?' I asked sharply. 'Don't you mean you *remembered* her voice?'

'No,' he said quietly. 'I heard her speak.'

My husband isn't given to fanciful notions. A forthright Dutchman and ex-marine engineer, he has no time for New Age astrology, reincarnation, meditation or even massage.

'What did she say?' I asked, stunned by his revelation.

'She asked me to walk over to Joan of Arc sitting on the mahogany table, and to look underneath. I did, and found a wad of fifty-dollar notes she must have hidden there. The moment I had them in my hand I knew your mother was happy because the weight lifted from my shoulders, and I was able to come home.'

I had read of visitations from the dead: mothers sending messages of love to orphaned children, sons asking for their parents' forgiveness – but never anything like this. And yet it was so typical of my mother. How could she have rested peacefully, knowing the money she had so carefully squirrelled away might end up in the pockets of strangers sent in to clear out her room?

A phone call

There's a television series called *Who Do You Think You Are?* in which celebrities discover their family history. Each time I watch an episode I'm surprised at how emotional they become during the journey, even though the stories are usually of distant cousins and long-dead relatives. Perhaps, as the title of the program suggests, learning about their heritage helps them understand not only where they came from, but also who they are.

Like the personalities on the show I too have relatives I know nothing about. And they include my father, of whom I have only the sketchiest knowledge.

Aware that our friend Colin has thoroughly researched his own ancestry, I mention to him that I've tried, without success, to find out more about my father.

'I can help you with that,' he says at once. 'The internet makes it easy to trace people now.'

I give him what little information I have. Within days he emails me the details of my father's birth. Armed with that information, I send off for his death certificate. Three weeks later it arrives from England.

After all these years I have an address! I Google it and see that my father lived in a unit; part of a large house in a leafy London suburb. I look to see who reported the death, hoping to discover the name of my half-brother, but the certificate has been signed by a woman – a woman who bears my father's surname.

I wonder. Could his other 'wife' still be alive? It's unlikely. He's been dead twenty years. His partner was probably of similar age to my mother and she's been dead for ten.

I give Colin the address and within hours he gets back to me with a telephone number. According to his information the place has never changed hands so it's possible my father's relatives are still living in the house. Colin suggests I call the number and find out.

I hesitate. What if my half-brother inherited the place when his parents died and it's he who answers the phone? What if he doesn't know about his father's other family? Should I tell him who I am? I don't want to complicate his life by giving him information he'd rather not hear. On the other hand, if I'm ever to find out why my father behaved as he did, I need to speak to someone who really knew him.

I decide to make the call.

When a woman answers, I'm disappointed.

'I wonder if you can help me,' I say. 'I'm looking for information about someone who once lived at your address.' I tell her my father's name.

'Waldo?' she says immediately. 'He's dead.'

Shock waves course through my body. She knew him! Could it be that I'm speaking to the woman who . . . My hand trembles. 'So are you related to him?'

'No, not at all,' she says firmly. 'I can't talk to you any longer. I'm very old, too old.' And with that she hangs up the phone.

I don't know what to make of it. Was she telling the truth? Something about the way she repeated my father's name gave me the impression she knew him well. I consider phoning her back, but I could tell from her voice that she was very old, and I don't want to harass or distress her.

So I haven't called again, and I may never know what motivated my father's odd behaviour. At one time I thought he was a wicked manipulator and my mother was his hapless victim. But as I grow older I no longer see black and white, only infinite shades of grey.

I'm not a subject of *Who Do You Think You Are?* and I don't need to know who *he* was, in order to know who *I* am.

Christine

I'm late. The plane has already landed and disembarking passengers flow past me as I rush to meet my old college friend. I know from our phone conversations that for her this journey is a huge undertaking. She's coming in from Sydney after a brief stopover, but has already flown halfway around the world in order to see me again. I should be there to greet her when she gets off the plane.

As I near the gate I see two airport staff standing by the desk, but there are no passengers. I'm about to turn around and go to look for Christine in the baggage hall, when a small boy walks through the door, clutching a teddy. He heralds the arrival of two weary families laden with nappy bags and baby bottles and after a short delay, a trickle of other passengers, three of whom are women travelling alone. None look familiar.

'Is that everyone?' I ask a stewardess.

She nods, and I hurry back down the corridor to the escalator where, briefly delayed, I rue the fact I didn't ask Christine for her mobile phone number. Then I remember it wouldn't work in Australia anyway.

In the baggage terminal people are jostling for position around the carousel. The first few bags are now appearing, so I'm sure Christine can't be far away. I squeeze between the passengers and their trolleys, searching for my friend's lively expression and curly blonde hair.

I can't see anyone who fits that description. Could she have been one of the first off the plane? What if she's already collected her luggage? What if she panicked when she couldn't find me and has gone off to look for a hotel?

I'm the only person around who has red hair. Surely Christine would pick me out if she were here? I scan the passengers' faces once more, mentally comparing them to the photographs in my album, pictures taken when we were last together – thirty years ago.

When that doesn't help, I circle the carousel calling, 'Christine, Christine,' softly at first, and then louder as panic overcomes embarrassment.

A woman stops in front of me and says, 'Hello, Sally.' She leans forward and kisses me awkwardly on the cheek. And then I remember seeing her earlier, at the gate. Experiencing no hint of recognition, I allowed her to pass by.

'How are you? How was the flight?' I ask, trying to overcome my confusion.

She leaves her bags with me while she goes to the rest room. I stare at the rucksack lying at my feet, wondering how this woman with the steel-rimmed glasses, straight hair and severe expression can possibly be Christine – that crazy, jolly girl with whom I whiled away my college years. Our occasional catch-up-on-the-news phone calls have meant nothing. I don't know this woman at all. She doesn't look like *my* sort of person, and I've invited her to stay with us for a whole month.

Just then she reappears, and knowing it's too late to do anything about it, I lead this stranger outside and introduce her to my husband who is waiting by the car.

At night over dinner, I confess that I didn't recognise her. 'You used to have curly hair,' I say, 'and you didn't wear glasses,' forgetting for a moment that these days I have to wear them too.

She grins. 'The curls weren't natural.'

I remember how she nursed a sick husband for years. She's a widow now. How could I possibly expect her to be the same bubbly, carefree person I knew so long ago?

Christine wants to see something of Victoria so we decide to take a trip down the Great Ocean Road, sightseeing along the way and sharing a motel room each night.

After a long drive we arrive in Apollo Bay. It's been Christine's first experience of the narrow winding road, and I know she's found our encounters with reckless drivers who encroached onto our side quite unnerving. It isn't long before we're ready for bed. We say goodnight to each other and turn off the light.

It's then that we find ourselves in college once more, sharing secrets about old boyfriends and giggling in the dark. And although we may look different in daylight, we discover that inside, neither of us has changed at all.

I show Christine my old college photograph and we pick out familiar faces and compare recollections of the years we lived together.

'I remember when you . . .' Christine says, and gives a detailed description of something *I* did, but don't remember at all.

We find it's mostly the small and apparently inconsequential things that are clearest in our minds. We talk about Big Bernie; how he found a swan lying dead in the snow and carried it around for days. He even brought it into lectures, until there was an outcry because of the smell.

We speak of harpsichord music and Handel, of writing poems about daffodils on yellow paper, and of drinking too much scrumpy in the Stable Block bar.

I remind Christine of the time we stood on the damp flagstones in Camellia House, watching the gardener cut flowers for us on Mother's Day. It was early March and not long out from winter – cold and grey. Inside the greenhouse among the leaves of those 200-year-old bushes, it seemed almost tropical. Whenever I think of it I smell the moist foliage and marvel again at the beauty of those exotic, crimson blooms.

Powerful memories have entered my brain through my nose. I smell fallen leaves and I'm a child again, picking up conkers and acorns on my way to school. I'm adding herbs to soup and find myself walking on a Greek hillside with wild thyme at my feet and the navy-blue Aegean far below. Strangely, fleeting moments I thought insignificant are fixed forever in my mind – and I've found that of all my memories, the sweetest are the saddest to recall.

Wakefield Press is an independent publishing and distribution company based in Adelaide, South Australia. We love good stories and publish beautiful books. To see our full range of books, please visit our website at www.wakefieldpress.com.au where all titles are available for purchase.

Find us!

Twitter: www.twitter.com/wakefieldpress
Facebook: www.facebook.com/wakefield.press
Instagram: instagram.com/wakefieldpress

Printed in Australia
AUOC02n1325110517
285622AU00004B/4/P

9 781743 054062